Woodcarver's Problem Solver

TRICKS, TIPS & SHORTCUTS

Graham R. Bull

Sterling Publishing Co., Inc.
New York

DEDICATION

To all of my students, who, together with their inquiring minds and their learning prowess,
have helped maintain the ancient spirit of woodcarving as a modern craft
for both the professional and the hobbyist

ACKNOWLEDGMENTS

Ken Hobson for gilded items, Don McKerrel for "Mirror Images," Malcolm Paisley for various tools,
Alberto Proietta for "posture," Vanessa Rowed for her hands, Bryan Smith for his lathe,
Linda Lubica Srank for "symmetry," Frances Taylor for various tools,
my mother Thirza for her hands, John Wigham (10 years old)
for "My Dad at the Beach"

Library of Congress Cataloging-in-Publication Data

Bull, Graham R.
     Woodcarver's problem solver : tricks, tips & shortcuts / Graham
R. Bull..
          p.   cm.
     Includes index.
     ISBN 0-8069-5892-8
     1. Wood-carving—Technique.   I. Title.
TT199.7.B86 2001
736'.4—dc21   00-048259

Book design by Judy Morgan
Editing and layout by Rodman Pilgrim Neumann

10   9   8   7   6   5   4   3   2   1

Published by Sterling Publishing Company, Inc.
387 Park Avenue South, New York, N.Y. 10016
© 2001 by Graham R. Bull
Distributed in Canada by Sterling Publishing
c/o Canadian Manda Group, One Atlantic Avenue, Suite 105
Toronto, Ontario, Canada M6K 3E7
Distributed in Great Britain and Europe by Cassell PLC
Wellington House, 125 Strand, London WC2R 0BB, England
Distributed in Australia by Capricorn Link (Australia) Pty Ltd.
P.O. Box 6651, Baulkham Hills, Business Centre, NSW 2153, Australia
Printed in China

Sterling ISBN 0-8069-5892-8

CONTENTS

PREFACE

The craft of woodcarving has been practiced since history began. Whether as a cultural record, as an income-earning trade, or as a craft to pass time, woodcarving's fortunes have been many and varied.

Today, many people in the world earn their living from their woodcarving skills, across a wide spectrum of styles from decorating fine furniture to creating tourist souvenirs. A vast number also practice the craft as a hobby, keeping alive, and indeed rejuvenating, interest in this manual art.

As with all crafts, time changes the tools and materials available to the practitioner. Language changes definitions, and new things emerge from changing technologies and manufacturing practice.

The objective of this book is to record those things that matter to the "modern" woodcarver. Some have remained unchanged for centuries, some are new. Many now redundant or otherwise impractical entries have been reluctantly excluded from the text.

The choice of subject matter for this record has been tempered by my teaching experiences over more than a decade. The content is a presentation of those aspects of tools and techniques that more than 1500 students have pondered and practiced. The subject of wood is covered only very superficially, this being the focus of another volume.

HOW TO USE THIS BOOK

This book must not be read as an historical treatise, but as a description of the tricks for skill improvement, tips on avoiding mistakes, and shortcuts available to the modern woodcarver.

Entries are in alphabetical order, most with an accompanying caption and illustration.

Where appropriate, the description for an entry contains cross-references to other entries, and these appear in CAPITALS. These cross-references are chosen to encourage searching out another trick, tip, or shortcut. By continually moving around the text in this manner, new pieces of information will be found, each helping you go one step further to a creative and fulfilling experience in the art of woodcarving.

Graham R. Bull
Sydney, Australia

ABRASIVE

There are many kinds of abrasives available to the woodcarver, each with different characteristics and some more appropriate than others for a particular task. If there is doubt, it is best to experiment on an offcut of the wood rather than risk damage to the carving. SILICON CARBIDE, PUMICE, ROTTEN STONE, GARNET, and ALUMINUM OXIDE are abrasives commonly used by woodcarvers. There are some basic principles that apply to most abrasives, and these are:

✔ Residual material such as sanding dust left behind in timber can be very damaging to carving tools, and the wood should be vacuumed or brushed thoroughly if further carving is required.

✔ Abrasives generally have a rounding effect on sharp edges and will "soften" their appearance; and if too coarse an abrasive is used, tearing and severe scratching of the surface may result.

✔ Working an abrasive in the direction of the GRAIN may assist in minimizing scratching.

ABSTRACT

See A–01.
In art, the abstract work is one that seeks to create an effect through form or shape, without necessarily being specific. The form may more or less reveal aspects of the specific subject that allow it to be "recognizable," or it may leave the interpretation completely up to the viewer and his or her imagination. In A–01 the abstract "MAN" is recognizable, albeit the proportions are incorrect, and age, race, and sex are not recognizable.

A–01
The degree to which an abstract work is recognizable is completely the will of the artist. To label it as in this case with the title "MAN" may be, from the point of view of language, to remove it from the abstract and make it a poor rendition of reality.

ACROSS THE GRAIN

See A–02.
Grain "direction," including AGAINST THE GRAIN, refers to the direction the CELLS are arranged in the wood. If the tool is pushed into the cells at any angle between zero and 180 degrees to the lie of the cells, this is cutting across the grain. Diagonally across would be at an angle of approximately 45 degrees. The majority of cells form in such a way that they lie in the direction along the branch or trunk of the tree. There are some, such as the "medullary ray" cells, that form across the branch or trunk. These are visible to the naked eye only in a few species such as oak (*Quercus* spp.).

A–02
A tool pushed in the direction of the arrow on the left of this illustration would be moving across the grain, and one moving in the direction of the arrow on the top of the illustration would be moving with the grain.

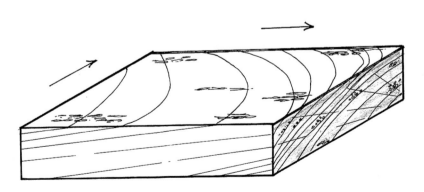

ADZE

See A–03.

An adze is an ancient tool, either with a long or short handle as is the case with a bench adze. The blade may be straight or curved and is generally at right angles to the handle. It is used to flatten the surface of roughly cut or axed boards. Depending on the shape of the cutting edge, it will leave a textured surface giving a "rough-hewn" look. This is sometimes a desirable effect for tabletops and other furniture.

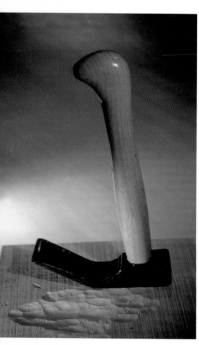

A–03

This bench adze has a shallow curved blade and will create a rough-textured surface.

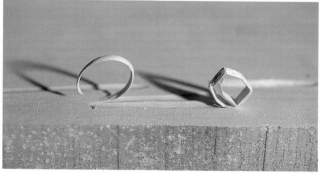

A–04

The wood curl on the left of the illustration has been made by a tool cutting with the grain, and the curl on the right with a tool cutting against the grain.

AGAINST THE GRAIN

See A–04.

When the tool is pushed into and along the CELLS of the wood and they break, split, or otherwise do not cut cleanly, it can be reasonably assumed that the tool is cutting against the grain. The tool will be digging into the ends of the cells rather that cutting cleanly through them, and they will break and split. Carving with the grain, on the other hand, will produce a smooth unbroken surface. If your tool creates a broken and messy cut in the wood, try altering the direction of the cut until a smooth result is achieved. Ensure also that your tool is HONED, for a blunt tool

may create a similar result. Cutting ACROSS THE GRAIN may produce a curl; however, it will fall apart easily as the cells have been sliced through and they will "disintegrate."

ALCOHOL

Alcohol is usually used in the workshop in the form of the clear, water-like liquid methylated spirits. It will have been tainted during manufacture to make its odor and taste unpleasant to drink. It is a solvent or thinner for some wood stains, modern surface "VARNISH" finishes, and older ones like SHELLAC. It is highly flammable and must never be used as an accelerator for things like wood fires. It is also very handy as a "grain raiser" when preparing a surface for finishing. Smooth with ABRASIVE paper or a scraper, for example, and then dose with "metho" (it evaporates quickly), and it will swell and raise the ends of the cells and you can smooth them off for an even finer finish.

ALIGNMENT

See A–05 and A–06.

In woodcarving, this may refer to the direction of the SHAFT of a tool in relation to the

A–05

The blade of this tool is out of alignment with the axis of the handle. Care and patience are needed when boring the hole in the handle to accommodate the tang of the blade.

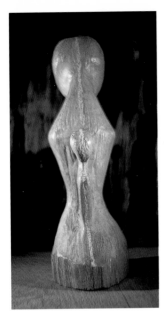

A–06
A centerline is an excellent aid for measuring to ensure requirements of symmetry or the correct location of carved features.

handle, where the shaft, or tang, has not been inserted into the handle in the direction of its axis. This will not necessarily hinder the performance of the tool, but may irritate the carver more than anything else. Poor alignment such as this may also reduce the life of the handle if a mallet is frequently used, as the distribution of stress will be more across the handle than straight down it. Alignment of a different kind is also an important feature of the carving process, ensuring that SYMMETRY (or non-symmetry as the case may be) is achieved. In this case a centerline down a model is an important reference from which measurements of alignment can be made. A FOCAL LINE is also used for the same purpose.

ALLOY
An alloy is a mixture of a main ingredient plus others, and "alloy steel" is a common tool term, which means, in effect, that STEEL, itself iron alloyed with carbon, is mixed with other things that are there to alter its characteristics. Alloyed with chrome vanadium, for example, steel becomes much harder, and sometimes more brittle. This combination is sometimes used for carving tools.

ALMOND OIL
A salad dressing for wood? Why not? After all, it's natural! In ancient times nut oils were about the only oils people had, and they were used as a wood finish. Almond oil is one of these, and is a clear liquid with a very slight odor and a mild nutty taste; it will impart a natural oil look to wood. It will soak in fairly easily, and it may take many layers, with drying time in between, to build up a low sheen. It is extracted from the seeds of the *prunus amygdalas*. Other excellent finishing oils are TUNG OIL and LINSEED OIL. Oil finishes are great for carvings where little sheen is wanted. Layers can be built up as needed to achieve the desired level of shine. Rags soiled with natural oils should be disposed of carefully to prevent SPONTANEOUS COMBUSTION. OLIVE OIL is commonly used as a finish for kitchen utensils.

ALONG THE GRAIN
See AGAINST THE GRAIN.

ALUMINUM
A piece of aluminum sheet can be used as a STROP for a fine edge on tools. Aluminum is the fastest of the metals to OXIDIZE, and ALUMINUM OXIDE is an excellent abrasive for tool polishing as a part of the HONING process. While the surface of the aluminum sheet may look clean, there will be a very fine film of the oxidized metal on it, and this will polish the tool.

ALUMINUM OXIDE
See A–07 and A-08. This is an abrasive substance used in many applications. For the

A–07
Aluminum oxide is a grayish powder. If you handle abrasives of any kind, be sure you do not breathe them in or ingest them, and make sure they do not come in contact with eyeglasses as they will cause significant damage to lenses.

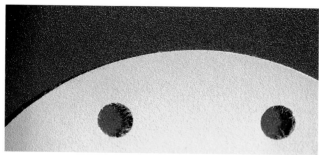

A–08
Aluminum oxide abrasive paper is mostly whitish, but can also be red-brown. It is an excellent abrasive for wood, cutting cleanly and crisply.

woodcarving process, it can be used in the form of powder applied to a STROP for tool polishing, or as a "sanding" paper for smoothing the wood surface. Aluminum oxide is an excellent wood abrasive, cutting cleanly and efficiently. Many different "grain" sizes are available, commonly from around "80 grit" to "1000 grit."

AMBIDEXTROUS

To be equally competent with your left hand as your right is an extremely useful skill to master, particularly where your BENCH may be up against a wall. It will save you having to turn your work around all the time, removing and replacing your CLAMP

continuously. If your bench is freestanding, it will also save you a lot of walking around in circles. With woodcarving, there is a lot of changing directions with your chisel strokes, and to be able to swap hands readily is a great convenience. The best time to "train your brain" to become ambidextrous is when you just start out with your new activity. While your brain is "scrambled" trying to work things out is the easiest time to train it to do new things. You will most likely find handling a mallet in either hand the hardest, so start using it left-handed if you are right-handed and vice versa from the very beginning. You'll see just how easy it becomes!

ANTIQUE

An historian divides time into "ages" or "periods" that generally reflect the commonality of certain criteria, which for the woodcarver will mostly be a particular design style, such as the Jacobean or early Stuart period from AD 1603 to 1625. An "antique" is an object from a period earlier than the current period. For the year 2000, an "antique" would be Victorian or earlier.

APSE

See A–09.
An apse is a projection and has slightly different definitions in art and architecture; however, for the woodcarver one of the few times an apse will be confronted is with Gothic tracery. In

this case, the apse is the projection between the foils, which are the curved portions of the design.

ARC

In geometry, an arc is a portion of the circumference of a circle. In drawing generally, it may be a curved line, whether of a circle or not. It is important—if the design calls for circular components, such as in Gothic tracery—that the carver be very careful to deliver just that. If they are to be portions of an ellipse, then so they should be. Uneven curves and crooked "straight lines" will be very obviously wrong and out of place and will detract from the appearance of the work.

A–09
The carver in this illustration is carving around the foil toward one of the four apses, each of which points toward the center.

ARCHITRAVE

See A–10.

An architrave is a term from the building and architectural industries, and is that part of the structure that forms the surround of an opening such as a door or a window. The modern architrave is a plain and often featureless wooden strip used as a trim to cover plaster and framework. Some modern doorways have no architrave at all. In ancient times, however, the woodcarver may have heavily decorated an architrave.

ARKANSAS STONE

See A–11.

A variety of marble-like stone mined in Arkansas in the United States is often used for

A–10
Carving such as this elaborate molding was sometimes used to decorate the architrave around doorways and windows.

tool SHARPENING. It is cut to various shapes, some of which are SLIP STONES, and is used, together with a lubricant, for shaping the BEVEL on tools. This stone can be cut to a very fine and smooth surface and is ideal for fine sharpening before stropping. It is non-porous, durable,

and very hard. It is often shaped for specialist applications such as sharpening the inside of a "V" TOOL and the inside curves of a GOUGE.

ARTHRITIS

See A–12.

This potentially serious and painful medical

condition affects the finger joints, and may make it difficult if not impossible for the carver to hold the handle of a mallet. Carving a very soft wood, instead of harder ones, and modifying the shape of the MALLET may make woodcarving possible. Alternative soft timbers that could be tried include Jelutong (*Dyera costulata*), Cheesewood (*Alstonia scholaris*), Aspen (*populus* spp.), Lime (*Tilia* spp.), or Basswood (*Tilia* spp.). Instead of a long-handled mallet, try one which has a finger grip only, and fits inside the palm of the hand. If there is any doubt, seek professional medical advice.

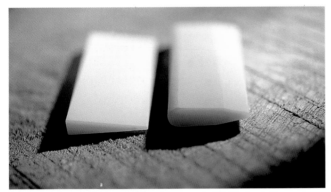

A–11
There are many different types of abrasive stone available for sharpening, and generally the finest grades are the only ones that should be used on carving tools.

A–12
A "palm mallet" such as this may make carving easier for arthritis sufferers, as there is no thin handle to grasp.

ATOMIZER

A simple spray pump on a bottle, purchased from your local market, can be very useful when you are carving wood that is very dry and crumbly on the surface, or when it is "WET" and you want to stop it drying out too fast. Use a spray pump like the kind used for spray cleaner refills. Wetting the surface of the wood with a mist of water will help make it easier to carve if it is very dry, and generally will not affect it in any other way. Keeping the wood damp if it is unseasoned will help save it from cracking. Watch for mold growth if you use the spray frequently.

BACK BENT

See B–01.
The shaft is bent backwards, and the BEVEL is on the topside on a back bent tool, which is also sometimes known as "reverse bent." This tool is for getting up under awkward places. For example, it can be used for undercutting where there might be a foliage pattern that calls for hollowing the under-

B–01
The back bent or reverse bent tool is not often used; however, it is useful for reaching up and under into awkward places.

side of a leaf where it overhangs a panel, such as on a cuckoo clock. The SHARPENING principles are the same as for a regular tool.

BAIZE

Baize is the felt-like covering commonly used to cover the playing surface on the tops of billiard and pool tables. Baize is available in different thicknesses and colors, and is made from natural fibers, although synthetic fabric is also manufactured. In wood work, it is used as a lining for drawers, particularly in jewelry or cutlery chests, and for woodcarvings it is an excellent material to place underneath so that the wood doesn't scratch the tabletop or other surface it rests on. Over time baize may rot, and it is susceptible to moth attack. "Craft" glue suitable for paper or cardboard is also suitable for fixing baize into place.

BAND SAW

Of all the electrical machinery available to the modern woodcarver, the band saw is arguably the most valuable. If there is

ever a machinery purchase decision to be made, this should probably be the first acquisition. It will be necessary to consider, apart from budget, the particular needs the carver may have with regard to the depth and width of the cut of the machine. Too limited a depth (say 2 to 4 inches, 51 to 102 mm) and the carver will be restricted to RELIEF CARVING and very small objects, unless blocks are built up by LAMINATING. CARVING IN THE ROUND will most likely require a minimum depth of 6 inches (152mm), and 10 to 12 inches (254 to 305mm) is ideal.

If there is a doubt as to the worth of the machine that falls within one's budget, the best advice is: don't purchase it. Better to use someone else's equipment and get satisfaction (even if this costs a little) than to spend capital and be unhappy with the end result. Always stretch the budget as far as possible and purchase the machine with the largest cutting capability. No band saw ever seems to be big enough!

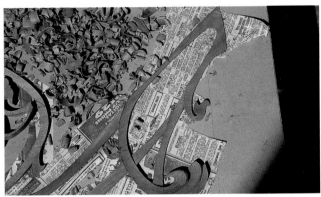

B–02
Scrap ply, particleboard, or solid timber with a couple of screws or just glue and cardboard forms the simplest and cheapest holding device of all. Many commercially available devices have limitations making them unsatisfactory.

BASEBOARD
See B–02.
Of all the devices, the simplest is often the best, and with a baseboard they don't come any simpler. Attach a RELIEF CARVING to the board with water-soluble glue and cardboard or even newsprint or a carving in the round with two screws from the bottom up. CLAMP the board to a tabletop—and there is the cheapest holding device of all. Use only water-soluble glue for the card or newsprint. When the carving needs removing, prize it off with a spatula or something similar. If there is paper left that won't easily peel off, dampen it and let the glue dissolve. For CARV-ING IN THE ROUND, use two screws, otherwise the carving is likely to swivel around with the screw acting like a pivot.

BEETLE
A beetle is a wooden mallet with a straight handle and a cylindrical head, with the handle connected through its side. The choice of timber for the handle is best made from a species that is a little flexible, as it might otherwise fracture and be jarring for the user. For the head, a species that will sustain prolonged end-grain impact without splitting is best. This style of MAL-LET is not particularly suitable for woodcarving; however, it is appropriate for tent pegging.

BENCH
See B–03.
There are as many designs for benches as there are ideas. There are, however, certain principles that if followed will make a very suitable carver's bench:
✔ Unless there is a specific need, make the bench square rather than rectangular. This will be more convenient to move around.
✔ Ensure the height of the upper surface of the bench is such that when the carver is standing upright in front of it, the palms of his or her hands rest on the surface when the forearm is parallel with the ground.
✔ Ensure the top of the bench is very rigid and does not flex or vibrate with blows from the heaviest MALLET the carver will use.

B–03
A square solid bench makes an ideal carver's workstation. Check the height for comfortable sitting and/or standing to prevent backache.

✔ Ensure the structure of the legs is sturdy enough to support the strong (and probably heavy) top, and that that framework is satisfactorily braced so it does not move or vibrate under pressure from the mallet.

✔ It is a good idea to have a foot rest for your own comfort. This could double up as a shelf to store tools on.

BENCH DOG

See B–04 and B–05.
A bench dog is a simple device that protrudes from the surface of the bench as a stop for resting timber against. One dog is placed on the tail stock of the bench and the other on the main table, and a perfect

B–05
This bench dog fits down below the surface when not in use, and the metal strip spring holds it up for adjustment to the height of the panel.

cramp is created for holding boards for relief carving. Tighten the BENCH SCREW to hold the carving steady. Dogs may be stored within the bench by making them rectangular in CROSS SECTION so that they can be re-

moved, turned side on, and a notch in the top used to stop them from falling back through. A metal or thin wood strip for a "spring" can be attached to the side so they can be placed partway into the hole in the bench without falling all the way down.

BENCH HOOK

See B–06.
Here we have another of the simplest yet most useful of holding devices. Made from radiata pine (*Pinus radiata*) or similar, the bench hook can be glued or screwed together. Use and abuse it, and clamp it to the BENCH if needed. For cutting wood and carving it, the bench hook is a most convenient disposable accessory. Make different sizes for different applications, and be sure the CLEAT that is held against the bench is not too shallow—otherwise it might jump off the edge of the bench. Make the top cleat just short of the width of the base, and it can be used as a cutting guide for a tenon SAW.

B–04
Clamp the carving between two bench dogs and tighten the bench screw. A long, rectangular bench with dogs is ideal for carving long panels such as signs.

B–06
Glue the cleats in place on a bench hook rather than using screws, which can work loose with constant banging.

BENCH SCREW

See B–07.

Another traditional holding device, the tail stock of a bench is moved in and out of the end of the bench by the bench screw. In days gone past, the bench screw was made from timber threaded and tapped, and lubricated with soap. If you make your own bench screw, it is best to use a "slow" thread, say of 8 threads to the inch. This will allow the jaw to move in and out slowly, increasing your control while adjusting the carving in place.

B–08
The right-hand half of this bench stone has been cleaned with kerosene and scrubbed with detergent. The left-hand side is clogged with dried lubricant and metal particles. It will not cut the tool steel unless it is clean.

BENCH STONE

See B–08.

A bench stone made for sharpening is not a good proposition for wood-carving tools. A SLIP STONE is far superior. Bench stones are most useful for constant angle sharpening of cutting edges such as those on hand planes and carpenter's chisels. For the carver, a stone that can be held in the hand is best. Bench stones can be used with lubricants such as machine oil or water.

BENCH STOP

See B–09 and B–10.

A bench stop is a simple device that stops the timber moving along the bench if it is being planed or carved. Some bench stops are threaded devices that wind down into the benchtop when not being used. A homemade bench stop could be a simple peg in a hole in the benchtop, or a hole bored in the benchtop could be used to house a plastic fitting purchased in the local

B–07
Keep the thread of your bench screw rust-free and well lubricated for smooth and easy operation.

B–09
This screw-down bench stop is a traditional "quick and easy" holding device.

13

B–10
The local hardware store might have easy-to-use removable plastic bench stops, or make one out of a block of wood and dowel.

tool shop. If the panel being carved is reasonably wide, it may be necessary to have two stops near each corner, and if it particularly long, it may be necessary to hold the other end in a tail stock using BENCH DOGS and a BENCH SCREW.

BEVEL
See B–11.
A bevel is a sloping edge, and the bevel the woodcarver is most concerned with is that on the carving tool. The bevel allows the sharp edge of the tool to be created, and its angle is critical to the behavior

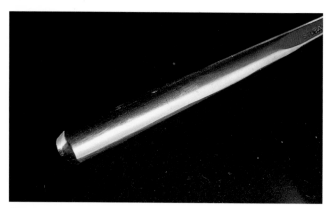

B–11
The shape and angle of the bevel on the carving tool is critical to the behavior of the tool. Harder and softer woods may require different bevel angles for optimum tool performance.

and performance of the tool. Shaping tool bevels with a GRINDING WHEEL is a skill that must be practiced, and it is important that they be ground uniformly and evenly without facets, otherwise the cutting edge may not be uniform. A long, thin bevel will allow a very fine sharp edge to be created, and this is especially useful for softer woods. The fine edge will tend to be inherently weak as it is very thin, and may not be suitable for harder woods, which may cause it to chip or SERRATE. A SHORT BEVEL that creates a thicker "sharp end" may be more appropriate in these circumstances and a SECONDARY BEVEL should also be considered.

BEVELED EDGE
See B–12.
A beveled edged tool is one that has a bevel running along the edge of the shaft. A carpenter's firmer chisel is traditionally beveled along both sides, making it more comfortable to hold and making the cut timber more visible above the tool, as opposed to the

B–12
A beveled edge on the tool shaft makes it more comfortable and sometimes easier to use, but it may also make the tool weaker.

carpenter's mortise chisel, which retains the full thickness of steel for maximum strength during the morticing operation.

B–13
This is the kind of hole-boring "bit" for a brace. There is often considerable tearing as the bit exits the timber, and it is not a particularly satisfactory hole-boring method for carving.

B–14
This screwdriver bit for a brace is an excellent tool for inserting or removing screws where extra purchase is required.

BIT

See B–13 and B–14.
A bit is a boring tool for making holes. It is used in conjunction with a BRACE to achieve high leverage, and is a tool from days past when power tools were not available. In today's language, the word bit is commonly used to refer to "drill bits" of all kinds. Metal twist drills, wood drills, doweling drills, and spade drills are all often called "bits" instead of "drills." For wood-carving, holes will not be bored very often, the majority of cases being when mounting carvings on backboards to hold them stable, or for piercing as in PIERCED RELIEF carving. Where it is undesirable to have tear-out as the drill bit comes through the wood, it is worth seeking out specialist doweling bits for doweling that have reduced or eliminated this effect. Sometimes when mounting a large carving in the round on a BASEBOARD, extra leverage is needed to insert larger screws. In these cases, the brace can be used in conjunction with a screwdriver bit for excellent and easy results.

BLUNTNESS

See B–15.
Blunt tools are the curse of the woodcarver. To achieve a finely honed edge is an art in itself, and practice and experimentation are important to achieve consistently fine edges. A very useful aid for the carver is the development of a "standard test" for sharpness. When SHARPENING a tool, the same standard can always be achieved if the same test is applied to each tool each time. A piece of soft wood that is unforgiving with a blunt tool is best

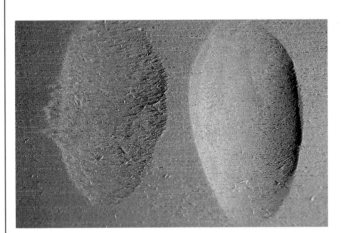

B–15
The cut in the jelutong (*Dyera costulata*) on the left was made with a blunt gouge. A far smoother result was achieved with the same tool after using a strop to hone its cutting edge.

to set up a standard test. Jelutong (*Dyera costulata*), basswood (*Tilia* spp.), cheesewood (*Alstonia scholaris*) or aspen (*Populus* spp.) are ideal. A blunt tool will tear the surface, make a grating sound, and require noticeably more energy to push it through the wood. If the tool is finely honed, there will be a crisp and clean surface finish, the SOUND will be clean and crisp as well, and the tool will easily move through the wood with no noticeable resistance whatever.

BORAX

Borax is sodium tetra-borate and is a mildly alkaline salt. Not used often in woodwork, it is sometimes handy for cleaning wood and for very mild bleaching activity, although it is not an oxidizing agent. There are more effective bleaching agents such as OXALIC ACID. Borax is used in laundry detergents as a cleaning agent, and is commonly used in art restoration work. It may therefore be an agent that might be tried for surface cleaning of old carvings. It is always wise to test cleaning and other restoration agents on "unseen" parts of the carving first, to ensure you are not about to set out on a path of further destruction.

BORDERS

Border decoration is a very ancient art. For the woodcarver, the most common borders will be for items such as picture frames, box lids, plates, and goblets. CHIP CARVING is often used for borders, while a picture FRAME can be quite elaborately carved and then finished with oil or WATER GILDING. A visit to the local art gallery is very worthwhile for inspiration in this area. Of vital importance for picture frame and other borders is the accuracy of the setting out of the pattern. The design for a frame must be able to accommodate mitered corners, and if the border design is a repetitive pattern, care must be taken to ensure the repeats fit neatly within the given length of the carved surface.

BOSS

See B–16.

A boss is a raised ornamental stud, which generally covers the intersection of moldings. In medieval architecture, a boss was a large knob or stud that held together the ends of the ribs of vaulted ceilings. They are to be seen in cathedrals and other buildings of the period. The boss was like a connector that stopped the ribs falling apart. Made of stone or wood, it was elaborately carved to decorate the otherwise unattractive item. For furniture, the simple ROSETTE or flower pattern makes an effective design for a boss.

B–16
The carved bosses in this wooden ceiling are anchoring the arched moldings together.

BOTANICAL NAME

The trees wood comes from have two kinds of name. First, there is the name you most likely call them, which is their COMMON NAME, and second the botanical name a botanist might use to clearly identify the tree as a particular member of a particular family of trees. Common names tend to vary regionally for the same tree, as they take up a colloquial or common usage. So a dogwood tree in the United States is quite a different tree from what is called a dogwood in Australia.

What the botanist tries to do is to classify a tree by a set of characteristics, so trees can be put together into families or species. It makes the study and identification of them much easier, and helps remove the confusion that is caused by common names. So the leaf, bark, flower, and seed become the botanist's classification tools. The botanical name may be made up of a species name, a botanist's name, a geographical name, a particular characteristic or the

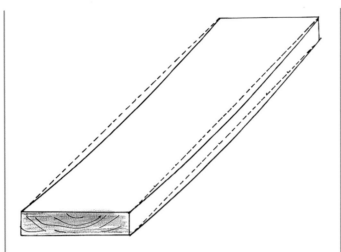

B–17
Always check sawn timber for distortion such as bowing, especially if the piece needs to fit within a frame or on a flat surface.

whole lot. The well-known North American hickory, for example, is in fact made up of four different members of the family known botanically as "*carya*," whose wood is a light honey color. At the same time, if you travel 400 miles northwest of Sydney, Australia, hickory is also well known, but it is a wattle tree botanically known as "*Accacia binervata*," with a dark chocolate-brown heartwood and cream sapwood. So you can see the confusion that could be caused if botanists didn't sort it all out!

BOWING
See B–17.
Bowing is a WARP where the board distorts end to end so that while the faces and edges remain parallel to one an-

other, they are no longer straight but curved. To see this distortion, sight the board along its edge. Carving timber should be checked for bow, particularly for long panels that need to fit inside frames.

BOW SAW
See B–18.
A very old style of handsaw in past times was made from a frame consisting of two "cheeks" with the blade held between the lower ends of the cheeks and between the tops a string which, when twisted, stretched the cutting blade to tighten it. Modern bow saws have a metal tubular frame and can be purchased from a

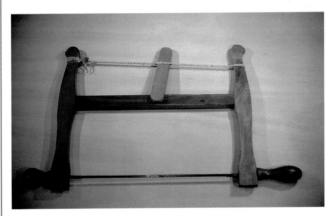

B–18
This old-style bow saw is more cumbersome to use than its modern counterpart. The temptation to buy at a secondhand sale should be tempered by a realization that it is probably of more use aesthetically as a decoration than practically for workshop use.

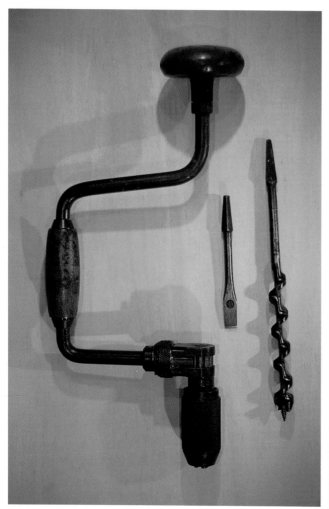

B-19
The brace allows considerable leverage for difficult situations such as removing stubborn screws or boring holes in harder woods.

to have the timber recycled for new carvings. A brace fitted with a screw bit can produce considerable leverage. Be careful not to sheer the head off the screw, in which case it will be necessary to drill away the metal of the screw with a metal boring bit. If this is to be done, first counter-punch the broken end of the screw, and then use a pilot pointed bit that will not slip out of the counter-punch indent.

BUILT-UP CARVING

See B–20.
The built-up carving technique is commonly used for carvings such as an elaborate picture frame. The design is broken down into its key elements and these are made separately and then assembled. This technique makes the "impossible" possible, and also in many cases simply saves considerable time and effort. Different-colored woods can be used for effect, and many layers can be fitted together. Restoration of such carved and assembled works can be difficult if everything is glued in place. During the design phase, thought should be given to the ease of dismantling in case of damage, and screwing parts in place may become a preferred option to gluing.

gardening supply store. The modern bow saw is a very effective tool for cutting branches and logs of green or dry timber, particularly for CARVING IN THE ROUND. It is lightweight and easy to use, and modern blades have a very long life.

BRACE

See B–19.
A brace is for use with a BIT that has a wedge-shaped four-sided shank. For the woodcarver, this system may be useful for removing screws that are very tight, such as in old furniture that is to be dismantled for repair or

B–20
This is a mockup of a built-up frame showing a common border pattern, the "berry and sausage," combined with notching, laid over a chamfered piece of rose mahogany (*Dysoxylum fraseranum*).

BUNDLE OF FIBERS

See B–21.

When carving along the grain, some difficulty may be encountered with regard to removing the waste wood, causing untidiness. This is because the lie of the cells in the wood is such that the tool is not cutting through them as cleanly as it might, like cutting AGAINST THE GRAIN. The tool is slicing along the cells and they are being lifted out in bundles that become untidy and difficult to remove. There is no easy solution, except to patiently cut through the ends of the fibers as best possible, ensuring very finely honed tools are always used. If there is ever a time when a blunt tool will do more damage than good, it is in this situation.

BURNISH

See B–22.

To burnish is to make something shiny. It is a common practice in art forms such as water or OIL GILDING, where gold leaf is rubbed with highly polished agate to increase its shine. For the woodcarver, it is not a commonly used technique; however, there may be occasions where the surface of the wood can be burnished to effect a low sheen. Some harder woods can be easily burnished, and generally softer woods cannot. For some waxy or resinous timbers, a very sharp tool will give a burnished effect as it cuts. To burnish wood, a hard polished metal surface would be rubbed over the carved surface until a sheen occurs. The only effective way to determine whether a wood sample can be burnished is to experiment.

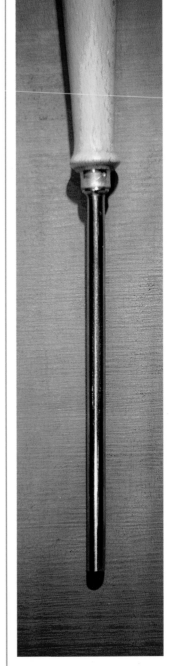

B–22
This burnisher is the kind commonly found in the workshop for sharpening a scraper. It may be tried for burnishing timber where the surface to be burnished is raised for easy access.

B–21
Cutting along the grain can often produce untidy carving; cutting across the grain is often the best approach.

BUTTER MOLD

A butter mold is a decorative wooden mold that is pressed into hardened butter to transfer a decorative pattern. The carving on the mold is done in reverse, or in the "negative," so that the pressed butter has the design raised, or in relief. The negative design is carved below the surface of the mold, and this is called INTAGLIO. Wood commonly used for these molds is boxwood (*Buxus sempervirens*), or other wood with fine grain that is easy to work. Fruit-tree woods like peach, pear and apple are good choices. If no wood grain is to be seen in the butter, carve on the end grain (on the end of the block of wood) rather than the long grain (on the side of the wood). End-grain Boxwood was once also a popular choice for WOODCUT printing blocks.

CALIPER

See C–01.
In woodcarving, a caliper is a simple but very useful measuring device for checking the equality of

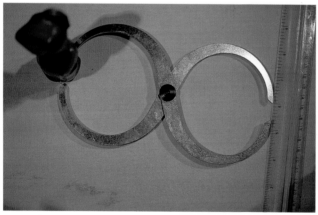

C–01
Double-ended calipers are commonly used in wood turning. They are also a very useful accessory for woodcarvers for taking awkward measurements.

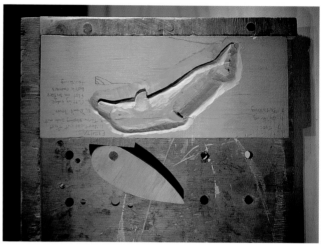

C–02
To ensure a firm fit for the dowel into the baseboard while allowing it to rotate, use a "fractional" drill no more than ⅟₆₄ inch more than the diameter of the dowel. Place a small piece of wood between the cam and the carving to prevent damage.

distances, in particular the thicknesses of the wood where it is being carved. It is important that the pivot of the caliper be firm or there be a locking device so the integrity of the measurement is stable if a number of thickness need to be checked against the caliper setting. A double-ended caliper as shown enables the thickness to be measured at one end while the measurement can be made at the other.

CAM

See C–02.
A cam is an eccentric wheel used in wood-carving as part of a holding device. It can be used on a BASEBOARD or BENCH HOOK that has a number of holes in it for positioning with different-sized carvings. This technique is ideal for uneven shapes. The cam in the illustration has a uniform curve; however, the pivot or axle is off center, creating the same effect as if the curve were eccentric. Make some "left-" and "right"-handed cams pushing the dowel axle through to one side or the other. The dowel axle needs to be a firm fit in the holes bored on the baseboard.

CANVAS

See C–03.

Canvas is a heavy cotton fabric that is sometimes coated to make it waterproof. It was the traditional sailcloth for ancient galleons of war and trading and fishing ships and boats. For the woodcarver, canvas makes an excellent TOOL ROLL for storage. Use a heavy gauge for best results. It has some moisture-absorbent qualities, and may help stop the formation of RUST. One design option is to sew into the roll-over flap some BAIZE to help protect the ends of the tools. The pockets should be large enough to take the handles of the tools, not the blades, otherwise it will be difficult to identify which tool is which unless the handles are marked all round. When reaching for a tool from a tool roll, care needs to be taken to avoid cut fingers.

CARBORUNDUM

"Carborundum" is a proprietary name. It is an abrasive used in cutting compounds and with a paper or cloth backing as an abrasive paper,

C–03
Waterproofed canvas is an excellent fabric for making tool rolls, and baize helps prevent tools from chipping.

and is made from the gray grit of SILICON CARBIDE. It is commonly used in grinding wheels, and comes in different-sized grains. 1000-grain silicon carbide is perfect for sprinkling on a leather strop to achieve a fine polish on tools.

CARCASS

In woodwork, the carcass is the body of a chest or cupboard, before it has its finishing parts included. For example, a chest without the carving, handles, hinges, lock, and surface finish is known as the carcass. The woodcarver works with the cabinetmaker to ensure that the carcass is made in such a way that carving can indeed be attached to it, or carved into it if that is preferred. The thickness of the timber panels, for example, should be agreed on with the carver before the cabinetmaker assembles the carcass for carving.

CARNAUBA

A wax obtained from the leaves of the Brazilian palm *copernica cerifera*. Carnauba wax is the hardest of the natural waxes. It is generally used as an additive to furniture polish, to give a harder, more durable and shiny surface finish. Its color will depend on the degree to which it is refined, from a natural medium brown to a light yellow.

CARPENTRY

Carpentry generally refers to a workman who builds or repairs wooden articles or the wooden parts of buildings. Its origins are in the Latin language, in which a *carpentarius* was a wagon maker, and the two-wheeled wagon was a *carpenium*. A woodcarver, on the other hand, may well have a variety of carpentry skills; however, he/she is generally concerned with the decorating of the surfaces that may have been created by the carpenter. It was of course not unusual in historic times for a carver to be employed as both carpenter and carver; however, the division of labor generally saw the carpenter prepare the work for the carver to decorate.

CAR POLISH

As a part of the tool SHARPENING process carvers will polish their tools to a super-fine edge. This is normally done on a STROP, which is mostly made from LEATHER, often with a very fine ABRASIVE coating. One of the most readily available and finest abrasives to be found is in the polish used for motor vehicle paint and chrome work. Spread a little on the strop, and polish to a magic edge. Check product ingredients lists, as some car polishes have no abrasive at all. TOOHPASTE may also be used on a strop.

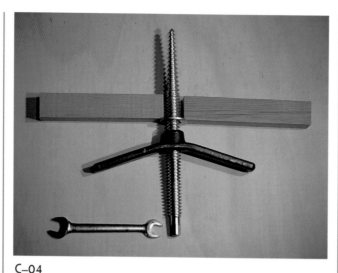

C–04
The carver's screw is placed up through the workbench, simulated in this illustration by the two strips of brown wood.

CARVER'S SCREW

See C–04.
This device requires a hole to be bored in the BENCHTOP, and the screw is inserted through the hole and then the small thread is screwed into the carving that is to be stabilized. The wing nut is then tightened on the underneath face of the bench. The carving can be turned easily by loosening the wing nut. Used for carvings in the round, the carver's screw is manufactured in different sizes. Large sculptural pieces would need a very large version for them to be stable enough for carving, particularly using a mallet.

CARVER'S STOOL

See C–05.
For the "Westerner" a bar-stool style is the most likely choice for seating in the workshop. However, for the professional Asian woodcarver, squatting on a mat on the ground is more the norm. For example, a Filipino carver might squat on a "dalapong" hewn from hardwood. It is just high enough to add a little comfort to the daily carving activities.

CARVING IN THE ROUND

See also the letter Q.
This is the term used to refer to carvings that are completed freestanding in the three dimensions of height, width, and depth. Whereas every object technically has the three dimensions, a carving in the round will be created to be viewed from any angle. A statue in the local park is "in the round" whereas a wall plaque of the same subject would be a RELIEF CARVING.

For carving in the round or in relief, neither one is more or less "dif-

C–05
This dalapong, or woodcarver's seat, is from the province of Mindanao in the Philippines.

C–06
In this sample of European oak (*Quercus robur*), which has been carved with a "cane weave" pierced-relief pattern, the cell vessels are clearly visible to the woodcarver on the chamfered edge and face of the weave, where they have been cut through and exposed by the gouge.

C–07
Seasoning and storage of timber requires great care to prevent permanent damage from checking.

ficult" than the other. They are different, and require the development of different skills. It becomes a personal preference as to which one, if not both, a carver might concentrate on. Generally a carving in the round will require development of superior visualization skills whereas a carving in relief will require the development of greater technical skills of shadow creation.

CELLS
See C–06.
Wood is made up of a collection of differently shaped cells or vessels that are hollow and are responsible for transferring the nutrients up and down the tree. Each species of wood is characterized by different cell shapes that lie together in a way peculiar to that species. The cell structure becomes the "fingerprint" of the species. Carving with or AGAINST THE GRAIN is a description of the direction in which the

C–08
This piece of Western Red Cedar has been badly chewed by a very blunt gouge.

chisel approaches the lie of the cells, and whether it cuts through them cleanly, or tears or breaks them out.

CHECKING
See C–07.
Checking is the cracking or splitting that occurs in wood when it is subject to the SEASONING process. It is the result of the shrinking or collapsing of the CELL walls in the wood as the water in them is evaporated. Checking is normally permanent damage. Checks may not always be on the surface of the wood, and the carver's nightmare is when a carving is in progress and all of a sudden there appears from inside the wood INTERNAL CHECKING that ruins the proposed design.

CHEWING
See C–08.
Chewing is wood damage that is the result of blunt tools and/or poor tool technique. Some woods are more prone to chewing in this manner than others. Woods such as Australian kauri (*Agathis microstachya*) and Canadian Western red cedar (*Thuja plicata*)

are good examples. They crumble across the end grain with blunt tools, and if a blunt gouge is rolled as in the making of a scroll, it will certainly chew the wood and cause significant damage. Poor tool technique such as twisting a gouge to remove waste rather than cleanly cutting the waste out will cause a chewed look. Positive cuts, sharp tools, and close rather than coarse-grained woods will help eliminate the possibility of a chewed, untidy appearance.

CHINAGRAPH PENCIL

Woodcarvers are always MARKING OUT their patterns on wood, and most often a regular graphite ("lead") pencil is used. Many times this is not all that successful, because of the color of the wood, or sometimes because LIGHT tends to reflect off the pencil line, making it shiny and hard to see. Chalk is not a good substitute, because it is powdery and can very easily penetrate the wood grain, discoloring it permanently. A more waxy marking medium is often better.

Often used for marking acetate overlays on maps, the Chinagraph pencil comes in a variety of colors, one of which will contrast clearly with the wood. The markings will not penetrate the cells too much at all, and can normally be scraped or chiseled off.

CHIP

See C–09.
Chipping is another form of wood damage that potentially has its origins in a variety of different areas. It may be the result of poor tool technique, blunt tools, incorrect choice of wood for the design, or poor design in itself. A chip in an unfortunate place can cause permanent dam-

C–09
The edges of this unfinished carving are badly chipped. In this instance chipping is caused by an incorrectly ground bevel and poorly honed gouge.

age and ruin the appearance of the carving. The chip may be glued back in place in an invisible manner, and if so this is more by good fortune than anything else. The approach of the tool into the wood is important to avoid chipping. For ex-

ample, if there is no support for the wood, as on the outside border area of a carving, push the chisel in towards the body of the carving, not outwards towards the unsupported edge. Avoid where possible very fine edges in the design. If they are important make sure the timber choice is of a close-grained wood that will cling together in very small cross sections. And make sure the tool is sharp so that it can actually cut instead of break the wood.

CHIP CARVING

See C–10.
Chip carving is a style of carving characterized by geometric patterns cut into the surface mostly using specialist tools

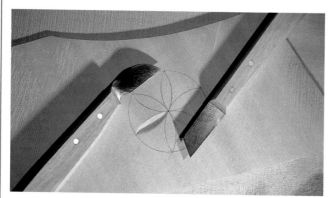

C–10
These are the two commonly used chip-carving knives. The knife on the left is a hook or bullnosed knife used for cutting the pattern. The knife on the right is a push knife used for making an incision to cause a shadow to form where the sides of the carving meet at the bottom of the cut.

called chip carving knives. Chip carving requires a manual dexterity high in accuracy for very fine work, to ensure curves and straight lines are neat and uniform. Chip carving is a form of ENGRAVING, and incised lettering is a derivative of chip carving. The best woods for chip carving are fine-grained soft woods, such as European Lime (*Tilia* spp.), American Basswood (*Tilia* spp.), or Asian Jelutong (*Dyera costulata*).

CHIPPED TOOLS

See C–11.
A chipped woodcarving tool indicates damage by dropping or banging, or breaking in the wood as the result of levering or twisting the tool, or using too finely ground a tool in too hard a wood. A badly chipped tool normally requires a GRINDING WHEEL to repair the damaged part, and this often means losing a considerable amount of tool steel and therefore carving life from the tool. If the chip of steel has broken away and remains in the carving it must be dug out and removed, otherwise the resharpened tool will

C–11
This "V" tool is badly chipped as a result of "levering" in a piece of hard wood. About ½ inch of tool steel will be lost when it is re-ground.

hit against it and most likely chip again. A considerable amount of chipping can be avoided if the tools are stored carefully in a TOOL ROLL so they do not bang against one another. Steel hitting against steel is a very common source of trouble. The advantage of a tool roll or a tool drawer for storage is that there are divisions between each tool. Make sure also that any holding device such as a VISE is faced with wood, to reduce the likelihood of the tool hitting the metal jaws.

CHIPPING CUT

See C–12.
A chip cut forms the basis of chip carving, and is in effect the making of a sunken pocket with the CHIP CARV-

ING knife like the petal in C–10. The knife is held in one hand, the wood in the other and resting on a knee for comfort, provided of course it is not too large. The hand holding the knife must be steady, and to aid this it is normally rested on the wood being incised.

CHISEL

A chisel is a cutting tool with a long blade and a sharpened end, normally a rectangle in CROSS SECTION, and fitted with a wooden or impact-resistant plastic handle. Traditionally, the carpenter used a chisel. A tool curved in cross section, which is the common carver's tool, was traditionally called a GOUGE. As language changes so does definition, and today the word "chisel" is generic for any shaped cross section. So a carver's "gouge" is commonly referred to generically as a "chisel." Chisels come in endless shapes and sizes depending on the intended use. They may be con-

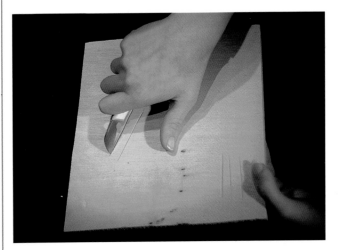

C–12
A comfortable posture is essential to produce the accuracy and neatness required for attractive chip carving.

C–13
This chisel chest holds four dozen tools in tray racks and has a tray for drawings, plus compartments for the most needed accessories.

ful not to transfer dirt from hands onto the carving. Polishing tools is the process of HONING and it removes very fine particles of steel from the cutting edge; and this discolors the polish with gray/black residue, which may permanently stain the carved surface. Always wash hands after using ABRASIVES.

CLAMP
See C–14.
There is a technical difference between "clamp" and "CRAMP." In wood-carving and woodwork, to clamp is to use a device (a clamp) to hold the carving in place while it is being carved, such as using a HOLD-FAST to secure the carving to the bench. To

structed in different ways such as with an external or internal FERRULE and a tang that fits up into the handle or a cone shaped socket that has the handle fitted into it. They may have a BEVELED EDGE, round edge, or plain EDGE.

CHISEL CHEST
See C–13.
A chisel chest is an excellent storage system for carving equipment. One disadvantage is that it can be heavy, depending of course on how much is in it and how big it is. Include trays that separate the tools from one another to prevent damage, and ensure there is somewhere to place the

MALLET, SLIP STONES, and lubricant. The handles on the chest must be strong and not likely to come loose. Strong hinges are essential for the lid. Chisel chests collect dust and shavings and need cleaning out frequently. Place a sachet of silica gel crystals in each tray to help prevent RUST forming on the blades.

CHROME POLISH
There are a variety of chrome polishes, and other metal polishes for brass and silver that could be tried on a STROP, some more or less abrasive than others. If a polish like any one of these is used, be care-

C–14
Strong good-quality clamps are essential for safe workshop practice. To prevent damage to the carving, place a small scrap of timber between the clamp jaw and the work in progress.

cramp is to hold pieces of wood together while they are being glued to form a block or a panel. In modern language, clamps and cramps are often described generically as "clamps." It is reasonable to speculate that the word "cramp" will disappear from common usage altogether. In woodcarving, there are numerous clamps designed to hold the carving, each clamp with different features. Here are some important principles to observe when deciding which clamp to purchase:

✔ The clamp must be strong and solid enough to hold the work still, often a problem with large carvings in the round.

✔ The clamp must be manufactured to a quality so that it does not come accidentally loose. Injury can result if a large clamp falls on the foot or leg.

✔ If the clamp has a screw thread, it is easier to use if it has a "slow thread" so that when it is wound it does not open or close too quickly. This makes for better and safer control.

✔ The material used in the manufacture of the clamp must be strong enough to take reasonable pressure without breaking or bending under stress.

CLAY

See C–15.
For the carver, clay is a potential medium for making a MAQUETTE or a model, before undertaking the actual carving in wood. Clay is easy to work in its wet form, but is prone to shrinkage and breaks easily when it is dry. It must be kept moist between modeling sessions, because once dry it cannot be easily reconstituted. There are different grades of clay

C–15
This clay is superfine with no gritty "fines" in it. Not all clays are suitable for modeling.

available, some not suited to MODELING, and the supplier's advice should be sought as to the best local clays available for this purpose.

C–16
Gluing is often better than screwing cleats to boards, as screws may work loose with constant jarring.

CLEAT

See C–16.
A cleat is a type of holding device and is nothing more than a piece of wood fastened in such a position as to support something else. In woodcarving, cleats are often used for holding or supporting applications such as in the use of a BENCH HOOK. Simple ideas such as these are quick and easy, make use of workshop offcuts, and essentially cost nothing. A cleat fastened to the bottom of a board turns it into a handy extra benchtop when it is clamped securely in a vise.

COLONIAL

See C–17.

The term "colonial" applies to the period of time of the early colonization of a country or community. For woodcarving, it is therefore a period design style that will differ between countries, and is characterized in the majority of cases by simple unsophisticated decorative carving done with basic tools. In modern times, those wishing to enjoy nostalgia of older times often make "colonial reproductions" of furniture and the like. To achieve the true colonial look, the carver must be mindful of the nature of the simplicity of the work.

COLOR TEMPERATURE

Color temperature is relevant when we are choosing LIGHTING for the workshop. Light is mostly the end result of the generation of heat, and depending on the nature of the heat it will manifest itself in different colors. The sun, for example, tends to red. Fluorescent tubes, while they generate their light in a different way, also have assigned color temperatures, mostly tending towards yellow and blue. Filament light bulbs commonly used in homes tend towards orange/red. When choosing lighting, the color temperature can have an impact on what is seen. Compare the color of a piece of wood under a fluorescent tube inside, at night, to the color of the same piece of wood outside in sunlight.

COMFORT ZONE

See the letter Z.

Comfort zone for the woodcarver refers to the mental disposition towards the activity at hand. Frequently, particularly when starting out carving, we tend to be over-ambitious, and soon generate a discomfort with what we are doing and become disillusioned. It is important that we start at a "level" that is very relaxed for us in terms of our learning curve and dexterity, and maintain a level of comfort that challenges us without depressing and frustrating us by our inability! Buy tools as and when you think you really need them, for example, and build up your set gradually. Don't choose designs that are so complex that they become too frustrating, and don't choose timbers that are either too soft or squashy or so hard as to be "impossible." Experimentation is the best way to find your personal comfort zone.

COMMON NAME

A species of wood has a common name and a BOTANICAL NAME. Common names may

C–17
When carving a period reproduction, it is important to emulate the simplicity and sometimes primitive nature of the art of the time and place.

vary from country to country. For example, a dogwood tree in the United States is quite different from a dogwood tree in Australia. Names also sometimes vary from region to region within the same country. For example, the species *cryptocarya oblata* is known as either "silkwood" or "bollywood" or "maple" within the same 100 square miles in northern Queensland in Australia. It is important when trying to obtain a particular species that its botanical name is used as the reference wherever possible.

C–18

C–19

Considered casually, the illustrated leaf and flower arranged together as in C–18, on the left, is a more pleasing composition than the leaf and flower arranged separately as in C–19. Placed in a context, however, with a title such as "Broken," the composition of C–19 would be the more appropriate.

COMPASS

See DIVIDER.

COMPOSITION

See C–18 and C–19. The composition of a carving is the manner in which the components of the design are arranged to create the overall effect. A floral composition may consist therefore of a leaf and a flower, or several of each attached to a stem and so on. The attractiveness or otherwise of a carving will depend not only on the nature of the different parts of the design but on the manner in which they are put together. While the assessment as to whether a composition is good, bad, or otherwise remains largely in the eyes of the beholder and is therefore very subjective, it also often depends on the intended message from the artist.

CONCAVE BEVEL

See C–20 and C–21. The BEVEL for a carving tool should not be concave—also called

C–20

An inappropriate concave or hollow-ground bevel will be created if the carving tool is ground on the edge or circumference of the wheel. Hollow grinding is a requirement of a wood turner.

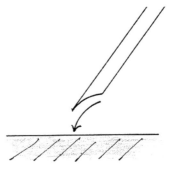

C–21

The concave shape causes the gouge to nosedive into the wood.

"hollow ground"—as this will cause the tool to nosedive into the wood, rather than push through and up out of it. A flat bevel is the easiest to produce when sharpening carving tools, although a marginally CONVEX BEVEL is often easier to use when carving. Concave or HOLLOW-GROUND bevels are used by wood turners on bowl gouges.

CONVEX BEVEL

See C–22 and C–23.
A convex bevel assists the exit of the tool from the wood and helps prevent it from nosediving into the wood. A SHORT BEVEL that is convex is suitable for carving deep curves such as a bowl, and a LONG BEVEL that is very marginally convex, are suitable for "normal" everyday use in medium-density timbers. A bevel that is too convex will be very difficult to use in most circumstances. Flat or convex bevels are created on flat grinding surfaces.

COPING SAW

See C–24.
The woodcarver will use a coping saw or a FRET SAW for removing the waste to make a PIERCED RELIEF carving. First it is necessary to bore a hole to accommodate the blade of the saw; then the blade, removed from the saw frame, is placed through the hole and refitted to the frame. An electric SCROLL SAW can be used instead of a coping saw.

C–22
Use the face of the grinding wheel to shape flat or convex bevels. Special wheels are manufactured for safe face grinding, where excessive pressure from large tools may cause the wheel to shatter at high speed. With carving tools, generally only very, very light pressure is used against the wheel, and in most circumstances a regular wheel is satisfactory.

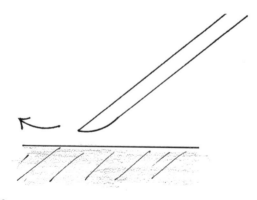

C–23
Be careful not to grind too convex a curve, otherwise it will be too hard to push the gouge into the wood.

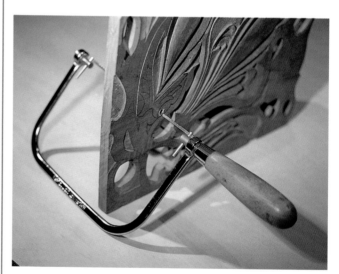

C–24
The coping saw is a useful accessory for any workshop. Blades may be inserted in the frame so that it cuts on either the push or pull stroke, and turned left or right so that they can cut sideways.

C–25
The corbels on this ancient building are an integral part of its architecture. They are the vertical scrolled brackets in the top half of the illustration.

CORBEL

See C–25.
A corbel is a vertical member that supports other parts of a structure such as a shelf on a wall, a mantel piece over a fireplace, or a bay window on a wall. They were and still are frequently elaborately carved. It is important to recognize that the purpose of the corbel is to aid in the structural integrity of the construction, and that the carving should not reduce its strength.

CRACKING

See C–26.
Cracking is breakage as the result of external applied stress, and in woodcarving is distinguished from CHECKING and SPLITTING. It is clearly of great importance that the woodcarver understand its causes. The majority of cracking is caused by:
✔ Incorrect positioning of clamps
✔ Over-tightening of clamps and vises
✔ Incorrect grain direction in relation to the design—for example, for maximum strength the wood grain should run along a carved animal's leg, not across it (for a carving in the round)
✔ Inadequate support in relation to the direction of the tool pressure—for example, an unsupported arm on a figure sculpture in the round may crack if there is no support for it when it is being shaped with a gouge and a MALLET

C–26
The cracking that is clearly visible in the center of this carving was caused by the grain direction running *across* the vine pattern and not *along* it, together with too much pressure from a cam on a baseboard.

CRAMP

See C–27.

A cramp, as distinct from a CLAMP, is a holding device specifically designed to hold individual pieces in place, especially while they are being glued together. Strips being laminated together for a benchtop are "cramped" together, often with a sash cramp. A window or picture frame might be cramped together for gluing up. If you are cramping up for gluing, be careful not to over-tighten and squeeze all the glue out of the seam. This is less likely to happen with softer woods than harder ones, as softer are often more porous. Check the glue manufacturer's instructions. If you are creating a wide panel for carving, be careful to ensure the panel doesn't CUP or

C–27
These boards will be used for a large carved panel. Note the scraps of wood between the jaws of the cramps and the wood, preventing damaged edges.

bend between the cramps. If each individual strip is perfectly square on the gluing edge, and the cramp is not over-tightened, this should not happen.

CROOK

See C–28.

A crook is a WARP where the board distorts along its length so that its edges remain parallel but are no longer straight. Before preparing timber for carving frames, borders, or panels, it is especially important the carver examine the pieces for distortion.

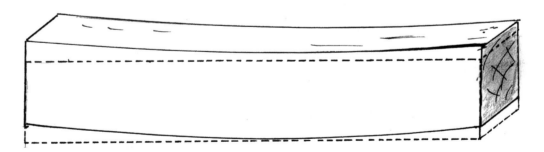

C–28
Distortion in wood like this crook can be caused by incorrect storage, inadequate seasoning conditions, or by natural stresses in the wood released when it is cut into a board.

CROSSHATCHING

See C-29.

Crosshatching is a design style commonly used to represent a roughly textured surface. It was traditionally placed on the stamen area of the Tudor Rose. Crosshatching is created with a "V" TOOL, SKEW, or knife. Care must be taken that the edges where the "grooves" stop do not break away or CHIP. It may be necessary to cut from the outside edge inwards to avoid this. If there is any doubt as to the ability of the timber to hold together without chipping, experiment on another piece.

C–29
Crosshatching in the center of this Tudor rose pattern was made with a "V" tool.

C–30
Without cross lighting, the chip arrowed in red would not be easily seen. If the lighting were vertical, it would not be noticeable at all. Refer to V–03, where this chip cannot be seen under vertical lighting.

CROSS LIGHT

See C-30.

Cross lighting in the carving environment is very important for the creation of adequate SHADOWS. Shadows enable the carver to see exactly what is being done with the tool in hand. They enable the carver to see the basic shapes that are being created, including mistakes that might otherwise go unnoticed. Remember it is shades of LIGHT and dark that allow shapes to be distinguishable in the first place. Unwanted cuts and chips are often not seen unless adequate cross light is available. A portable "reading" light that is not a fluorescent kind is best. Fluorescent tube lights are design to be non-shadow forming—they diffuse light rather than concentrate it. Cross lighting may be supplemented with VERTICAL LIGHT, but this is not essential. It is essential, however, to supplement vertical light with cross light.

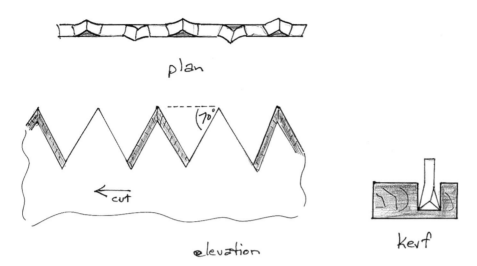

plan

elevation

kerf

C–31
The configuration to the teeth on saw blades has a major impact on their performance. Not only do they need to be sharp, they need to be the correct shape for their required task. This is the configuration for a crosscut saw.

CROSSCUT SAW

See C–31.
The majority of saws purchased for general woodwork are of the crosscut variety, as opposed to the RIPSAW design. The distinction is mainly in the design of the cutting teeth, which will be shaped and sharpened differently for either application. The woodcarver may well need one of each, particularly if wood is to be cut by hand from larger pieces. The crosscut saw is for cutting across the grain as in the case of cutting a piece from the end of a board, and the ripsaw for cutting along the grain as in the case of cutting along a board to make pieces for a frame. When purchasing a saw it is a good idea to specify which kind is needed, particularly if it is for ripping.

CROSS SECTION

The cross section of a piece of wood is the area of a "slice" through it, often bound by the width of the face and the height of the edge.

CUPPING

See C–32 and C–33.
Cupping is a WARP caused by wood CELL shrinkage such that the board curves between its edges. Often cupping can be prevented by the manner in which the board is cut from the tree. Quarter sawing, for example, results in the growth rings of the wood being aligned between one face and the other, and this generally reduces the likelihood of the board cupping. If the board is cut so that the growth rings are aligned between edges, the board is likely to cup towards the growth rings of greater diameter.

Cupping can also be a direct result of the carving itself. When a surface is carved in relief, con-

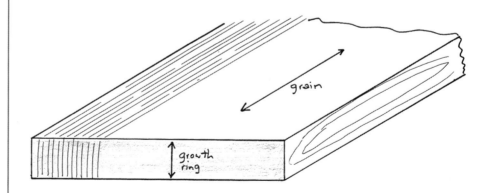

C–32
In this illustration the growth rings are at right angles to the faces, the board is therefore quarter sawn, and it is less likely to distort between the edges.

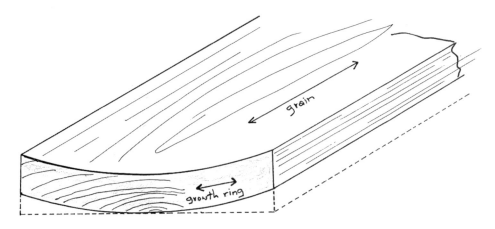

C-33
In this illustration the board has cupped between the edges and in the direction away from the narrowest diameter growth rings.

siderably more surface area is exposed to the atmosphere than when it is not carved. This may in turn cause the wood to dry more (and shrink) on the carved side than the flat side, and it may cup towards the carved side. For large carved panels it is a reasonable safety precaution to strengthen the flat (reverse) side with cleats to help prevent this movement. Screw them on rather than using glue, so they can be removed if necessary.

CUTTING COMPOUND

A cutting compound is an ABRASIVE mixture, and is often in the form of a paste. In carving and woodwork generally, there are many different abrasives used to alter the texture (mostly to make it smoother, but some to make it rougher) of the wood surface or the surface coating on the wood. Common abrasives include aluminum oxide, silicon carbide, PUMICE, calcite, ROTTEN STONE, and silicon. They may be used in pastes and liquids that come in the form of manufactured products like car polish, jeweler's rouge, toothpaste, chrome polish, brass polish, and silver polish. Some may be mixed with water to act as a lubricant and used with leather as an applicator. In carving, these sorts of manufactured compounds would be used on strops for polishing sharpened tools, or individual powders with water for fine cutting of varnished surfaces before re-coating.

DANISH OIL™

Danish Oil™ is a trade marked product manufactured under license in different countries. It is a surface finish that penetrates timber. It hardens the surface, has a low sheen, and imparts an oiled look. It can be used as a sealer under wax, which will impart a mellow look. Danish Oil is sometimes used as a generic description to refer to similar products, and this is strictly speaking incorrect. In most circumstances, one application of this product is sufficient, and wiping off the excess before complete drying will give a better result. Always follow the manufacturer's instructions. If applied with a brush, brush marks may well be visible if excess is not removed, or if two applications are made. Danish Oil together with beeswax furniture polish makes an excellent finish for a woodcarving. There are many other oils such as OLIVE OIL that are also appropriate surface finishes for woodcarvings.

DECORATIVE WOODCARVING

Decorative woodcarving is a term generally applied to the practice of decorating the surfaces of such things as furniture, or other items that might be used in conjunction with furnishing a room, such as coats of arms and other wall plaques. It consists mostly of RELIEF CARVING and is one of the oldest art forms in the world. It has been practiced to varying degrees by most races in recorded history, and excellent examples remain in many countries in cathedrals, museums, and private homes. Some very famous people were woodcarvers: Jesus of Nazareth, Abraham Lincoln, and Michelangelo. Being manually intensive, it is not often practiced today as a commercial proposition in its own right, except in some countries where carved wooden tourist souvenirs are common. Some countries with low labor costs, such as currently exist in Southeast Asia, export heavily decorated furniture to the more financially affluent areas of the world.

DEPTH GAUGE
See D–01.
This is a most essential accessory for the woodcarver, particularly for RELIEF CARVING.

Where there are large expanses of background a depth gauge will help ensure even cutting. Whereas small variations in depth may not be particularly visible, when transposed over larger spaces they tend to become greater without the progressing depth being noticed, so that from one side to the other depth variation may be quite significant.

DEPTH OF CUT
See the letter U.
One of the great mysteries when we start out carving is to work out just how deeply we should cut. Generally we are very tentative, and "pick around the problem," not progressing very far over long peri-

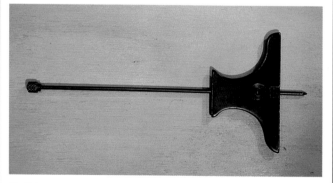

D–01
If a small depth gauge such as the one illustrated is difficult to use with a large carving, place a rule or straightedge across the carving from one side to the other and measure depths from the edge of the rule to the background.

ods of time. We are afraid that we will go too deep and destroy or badly damage our work. Certainly poorly controlled cuts that go too deep can cause significant damage, especially if they penetrate right through the wood. The best way to "get the feel" for how deep you can safely go is to experiment on scraps of wood. You will soon achieve an instinctive UNDERSTANDING and become so familiar with the apparent problem that it will disappear for you. It is also important that the carver come to an understanding about the angle of approach of the tool into the wood. The wrong angle will potentially cause more dam-

age than going too deeply. The angle of the bevel of the tool will influence the angle at which the tool will dig into the timber and this will influence how deep it goes, so this needs to be taken into account when assessing the angle at which you start your incision. Once again, this seemingly difficult problem of technique will soon offer instinctive solutions.

DIAMOND DRESSER
Diamond dust has long been used as an abrasive, and it is available to woodworkers in the convenient form of a DIAMOND STICK, and other SHARPENING blocks of various shapes that can be used for cleaning and dressing the surfaces of a GRINDING WHEEL and bench sharpening stone. The dust comes in different grades for different applications. A DIAMOND STICK with an industrial diamond mounted on the end of a steel rod is also available for dressing wheels. These require either an exceptionally steady hand or a tool rest for stable use, otherwise

there is a very significant risk that the diamond will dig into and badly damage the wheel. It is important to frequently check that the wheel surface has not become embedded with steel grindings from the tools, otherwise a situation will develop where steel is effectively grinding on steel—resulting in burning instead of cutting. Use the dresser to clean off these particles and restore a fine cutting surface.

DIAMOND STICK

See D–02.
Ideally a diamond stick should be used in conjunction with a jig to hold the stick steady. A smooth action with the stick across the face or edge of the wheel to be dressed is achieved by practice, ensuring the diamond stays at a constant distance from the center of the wheel for cleaning edges, and at a constant distance from the opposite side for cleaning faces. Remove only very fine "shavings" at a time. Dressing a GRINDING WHEEL creates reasonable amounts of very fine dust, which is a combi-

D–02
It is important to follow basic safety precautions when dressing a grinding wheel with a diamond stick. Considerable dust will be created and it is necessary to wear eye protection and a respirator or face mask.

nation of the compound of the wheel plus the steel particles from the tools. Wash your hands after using the dresser, to protect from transferring the dust to your eyes or the surface of eyeglasses, where it can do extreme damage.

DIAMONDING

See D–03.
Diamonding is a WARP across a square or rectangular CROSS SECTION of wood, particularly where the GROWTH RINGS are running diagonally across the section. This can be a major problem for carvings in the round if the wood starts to

move during the carving process. Ensure it is SEASONED before carving commences. If the carving is on a turned spindle (such as a candlestick), and the wood

begins to move, it may go into an oval shape. If there is a hole bored through the center of the wood, this too may become oval-shaped.

DIAMOND STONE

Whetstones using diamond dust as the cutting medium can be a quick and effective accessory for sharpening carving tools. They will not generally give the fine performance of a superfine oilstone or WATERSTONE; however, they are a good substitute for a fine grinding wheel used for basic shaping. It may take longer to cut the tool steel by hand; however, accuracy may be more achievable.

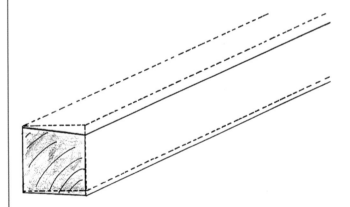

D–03
Even seasoned wood may move (change shape) as a result of changes in atmospheric conditions. "Diamonding" is a typical distortion.

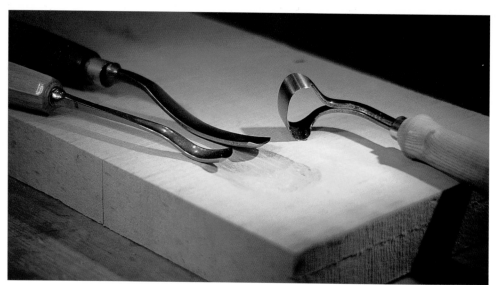

D–04
Different tools may be used for a similar end result. Experimentation with the tools available often reduces the necessity for another tool purchase. This spoon bit gouge, long bent gouge, and scorp can each be used for making dished shapes.

DIGGING

This is not an official term in woodcarving, except from the point of view that it shouldn't happen! The act of carving is, however, a digging motion. There is no doubt about that. Nevertheless, once the technical aspects of using the tool in the timber are overcome, it is the finesse of the execution that converts the "digging" into "molding," or "sculpting" and transforms the piece of wood into the carver's art. The process of carving becomes an act of the soul and is no longer the act of a digger.

DISH

See D–04.
Creating concave shapes is known as "dishing." Shallow dishing would be generally used for leaves, for example, and deep, concave curves become bowls. Various tools are available to the carver for these purposes. A shallow dish may be cut using regular straight-shafted gouges. Deep concave curves may be cut with long bent and short bent gouges, and there are specialist tools such as the SCORP that can be used for bowl making.

DISTRESSING

See D–05.
This is the act of damaging the surface of the wood to make it look "old and used." Distressing is often used in antique reproduction. This may take the form of physical damage to the wood to give it a knocked-about, abused look (a broken house brick can be used for this). It may be discoloring the wood by staining or other means such as rubbing or sprinkling with ROTTEN STONE to give a similarly aged appearance. Chemicals purchased from craft retailers can be applied to give a crazed appearance, a darkened or burnt look, or a variety of other effects. Always test the intended distressing method on something other than the finished work, and if there is any doubt as to the effect, then don't do it!

D–05
An old and dusty look has been imparted to this gilded cherub decoration by applying rotten stone to a coating of not quite dry shellac.

DIVIDERS

See D–06.

Dividers, also referred to as a COMPASS, are used to measure the distance between two points and then to transfer that measurement from one part of the work to another. By setting the locking device that is at or near the pivot, continuous equal divisions can be marked out for border patterns. There are different designs of divider available for the woodcarver; however, listed below are some of the key attributes to be observed:

✔ The points should be of equal length, made sharp, and be capable of being kept sharp. Brass tips are ideal for this.

✔ The points should be firmly fixed into the legs, so they do not move during use.

✔ The locking device must be firm and not easily moved once it is tightened, otherwise uneven measurements will result.

✔ The legs the points are inserted into must be of the same length for easy use.

DOG LEG

See D–07.

This tool is a specialist tool that will not be

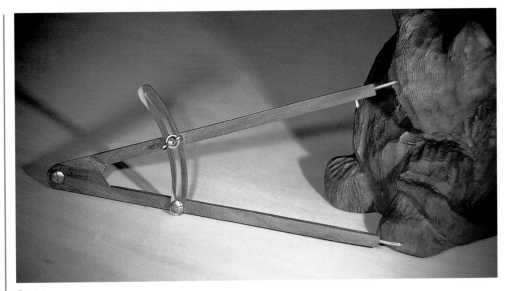

D–06
These dividers are made from gidgee (*Acacia cambegei*), an Australian inland desert wattle. It is a very fine and very dense wood, used by indigenous Aborigines for boomerangs.

used very frequently. It is flat in cross section, with the bevel on the topside. Flat tools (like carpenter's chisels) have the disadvantage that unless they are used with great care, the corners tend to make tracks in the surface of the wood. The dog leg carver's tool is used for flat surfaces like backgrounds in awkward places. It can also be used for undercutting in a way similar to the BACK BENT gouge.

D–07
Specialist tools such as the dog leg are not used often; however, they are very useful for awkward situations, particularly grounding.

DOLLY

A dolly is a platform on castor wheels for allowing large objects to be moved around the workshop. It is especially useful for moving around a large SCULPTURE. If it is used for this purpose, it is essential that a braking or locking mechanism is either an integral part of the wheels, or that wheel chocks be handy to stop the dolly rolling away when carving is in progress. Make sure the wheels are strong and can take heavy weights. Most wheels sold in retail outlets come with a load-bearing safety factor.

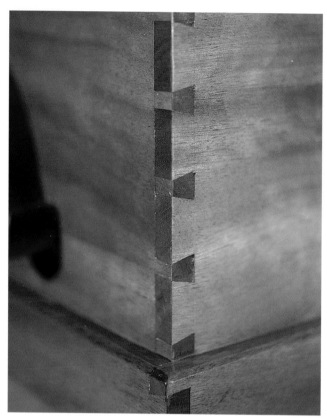

D–08
Carving into joints of any kind is best avoided. Not only is grain direction problematical, cutting into the joint and weakening it is most probable.

ternating grain will make the carving difficult if not impossible. The pattern may also look odd, as a result of the alternating texture of the joint. As a general principle, avoid carving over any JOINT.

DRAWKNIFE

See D–09.
Varying blade lengths and handle angles characterize this very useful instrument. The blade generally has a bevel on one side. Cut with the bevel down for easy-to-control cuts. This tool is excellent for larger works such as rocking horses and SCULPTURE. The blade length makes this a tool that

must be treated with great respect from the safety point of view. Sharpen it with a larger slip stone or a bench stone, keeping the fingers well away from the cutting edge.

DRILL

See D–10.
The word "drill" has become a generic for boring tools of different kinds, such as the wood-boring bit for timber and the high-speed drill for metal. There are many configurations of drill available for different purposes. Some are designed specifically for high accuracy for making holes to accept dowels, others for self-

DOVETAIL

See D–08.
A dovetail in woodwork is a specific join made to hold two pieces of wood together in a corner configuration. Because each alternate part of the join will be end grain or long grain, there is a regular alternating mixture of GRAIN pattern. It is best to avoid planning to carve on a dovetail joint, as this al-

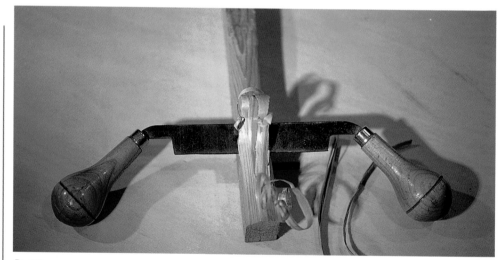

D–09
Store a drawknife with a protective strip of plastic or thick rubber material over the blade to both protect it and render it safe. A length of plastic garden hose with a slit down it is ideal.

D–10
This drill has a "pilot point" that centers the bit quickly and accurately into a previously center-punched mark.

made exactly where they are required, with no slipping of the drill.

EASEL
See E–01.
Most commonly used for the art of painting, the easel is a useful concept for relief carvers. It must be solid

centering for accurate positioning, and others such as a TAPER BIT for creating tapered holes for accepting the TANG of a tool HANDLE. Mark the position of the holes with a center punch (a punch with a pointed end) before drilling. For PIERCED RELIEF carving this ensures the holes will be

and stable enough to take the weight of the wood and any jarring from a mallet. RELIEF CARVING is mostly done with the board being carved clamped to a benchtop. In many cases, however, the carving will be displayed vertically, for example hanging on a wall. As this is the case, it is essential that during the carving process it be periodically removed from the BENCH and viewed vertically by the carver. It makes considerable sense therefore to consider the possibility of making an easel to

hold the work during its carving, thereby always approximating its final display position.

EBONIZING
Ebonizing is producing a black finish. "Ebony" is also a common name for a family of timber species. The wood may vary from plain black to black with brown striations. There are many different techniques that make a black finish, giving results from a mat to a "piano finish" (mirror-like). Commonly carbon black (lampblack) was used as a pigment added to SHELLAC.

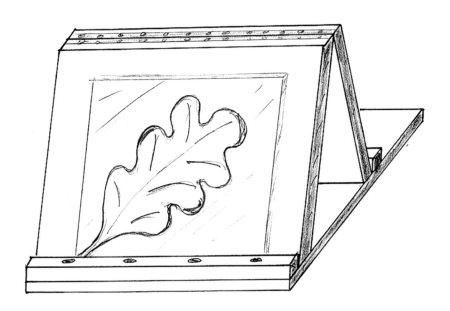

E–01
An easel for woodcarving can also be a very useful holding device for a carver with restricted movement, such as confinement to a wheelchair.

ECCLESIASTIC

See E–02.

Ecclesiastic means relating to the Church. Ecclesiastic carving includes such things as MISERI-CORDS, and bench or pew ends. Considerable history surrounds ecclesiastic carving, a large amount of which remains the record of history itself. From the prolific carving in major cathedrals to the simplest of decoration in the smallest churches, a carver interested in this subject has an endless supply of inspiration. The science of church architecture and decoration is called ecclesiology.

E–02
Ecclesiastic woodcarving offers an extraordinary range of study, the art primarily portraying the lifestyle of the time.

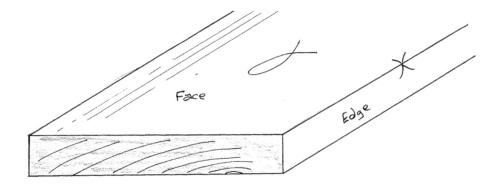

E–03
A planed or "dressed" face is often marked with an "alpha" symbol, and two surfaces at right angles to one another are often marked with arrowheads.

EDGE

See E–03.

In woodwork there are certain conventions with regard to definitions that save communication "confusion." Two of the most common are the EDGE and the FACE. The area between the two faces and the two edges is the CROSS SECTION. When communicating measurements, it is conventional to give the cross section first, with the face dimension (the width) before the edge (the thickness) dimension, followed by the length.

EGG & DART

See E–04.

This border decoration is common in pre-modern periods for furniture, frames, and mantel pieces. Repetitive alternate patterns require careful setting out and uniform carving. Other common repetitive alternate patterns that are still to be seen frequently are the bead, or berry, the sausage, and the ribbon and leaf.

E–04
This egg & dart alternating repetitive pattern is also known as egg and tongue. A bead and sausage can be seen in Illustration B–20.

ELEVATION

See E–05.

In drawing and architecture, an elevation is the projection of a building or other structure in the vertical plane. Similar to the conventions of face and EDGE, this convention is useful for identify-

E–05
Using correct terminology assists with the location and identification of subjects under discussion or those being planned for future making. This is the "north elevation" for the building.

ing parts of a structure that might need decorative carving. For example, carved gable ends may be required on the front or rear elevation of a building. These may, for example, be further identified as North elevation or South elevation on a set of plans.

ELLIPSE
See E–06.
An ellipse is an oval shape. It is the path of a point that moves so that the sum of its distances from two points is constant. To draw an ellipse

without any other available instrument requires two drawing pins, a pencil, and a piece of string. An ellipse is often the shape for a mirror frame that may need carving—an "oval mirror." As the carver advances with different kinds of work, a set of drawing instruments is a valuable purchase, including FRENCH CURVES, compass, and squares. A drawing board made from a softer wood, so pins can be used to hold paper, is also a useful acquisition.

EMBOSS
Embossing is the making of decoration so that the pattern is raised above the surface. Carving in relief is embossing. In more common usage, embossing is the imprinting of a pattern so that it is raised above the surface, such as on a business card or letterhead.

EMERY POWDER
Emery powder is a dark form of corundum (ALUMINUM OXIDE) used as an ABRASIVE. Rubies and sapphires are precious forms of corundum.

ENAMEL
A gloss surface finish mostly done with oil-based paint. In the past, enamel was a glassy, colored opaque substance fused to the surface of metals, glass, or pottery as a decorative or protective coating. If a high-gloss finish is to be used on a woodcarving, the carving itself will require specific planning. The carver must be aware that high levels of shine may reflect too much LIGHT and interfere with the visibility of the detail. If a gloss coating is required, it is important to

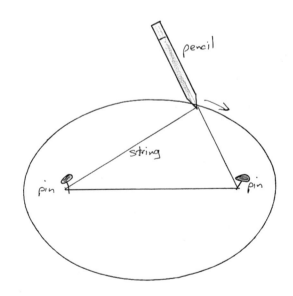

E–06
An understanding of basic geometry is of great assistance to the woodcarver for setting out and designing symmetrical patterns such as the ellipse.

carve the detail in such a way as to allow for the thickness of the coating, including any necessary "undercoats." It is conceivable that the thickness of such a finish could be up to $\frac{1}{20}$ inch (1 mm).

ENGRAVING

See E–07 and E–08.
Wood engravings are the basis for the making of relief prints. A wood engraving is also known as a woodcut. Designs are cut away as "valleys" below the surface of wood blocks. These valleys collect ink, which is transferred to paper by the application of pressure. Special WOOD BLOCK cutting tools are used for engraving. The choice of

E–07
Use the end grain if no wood grain is to show in a woodcut print. Fine-grain timbers are best.

wood for printing blocks will depend on the design effect required. For example,

E–08
This simple impression was made by filling the woodcut with thick printing ink, scraping off the excess, and pressing the end of the branch of peach wood into the paper.

if no evidence of wood grain is desired, then the end grain of a fine-grained timber is best. The smaller the cell vessels that are "opened" when the end grain is cut, the better. End-grain box wood was commonly used, although excellent results can also be achieved by using common fruit woods such apple and pear. Some of these timbers can be hard to cut, so it will be necessary to experiment to make the most appropriate choice.

EQUILIBRIUM

See the letters X and Z.
In woodcarving terms, equilibrium may refer singularly to the state of balance of a design, or the balance between the carver's disposition, tool skill, tools, design, and timber. For successful carving, it is these "things" that must be in equilibrium. Too high an ambition in relation to one or other of the elements may cause frustration, too low may cause boredom. The wrong tools, poor timber choice, impossible design and so on may also result in sufficient imbalance so as to make success an improbable outcome. Equilibrium can only be achieved with accumulated experience. Experience will be achieved by applying an inquiring mind to experimentation and practice.

ESCALLOPED

See E–09.
This is a design style taken from the outline shape of the scallop shell. It may appear in different forms, such as scallops on a table edge or patterns on a coat of arms, or variations in

any form. It is a common carving decoration of furniture of the Queen Anne period (AD 1702 to 1727 onwards). Shell patterns based on the scallop shell were common in mirror crests and chair backs.

ESCUTCHEON
See E–10.
For the woodcarver, an escutcheon may be the panel on a ship's stern bearing its name or a plate for protecting or ornamenting the keyhole of a door. In both cases, they were sometimes carved wooden adornments. In modern times the escutcheon for a door keyhole is more likely to be a metal plate.

E–10
To decorate the modern home's front door with a carved wooden escutcheon plate would certainly make a distinctive entranceway.

When producing these carvings, weather conditions need to be taken into consideration when choosing the wood. Teak is a popular choice for exterior ship carving as it is naturally weather resistant. Other choices might be kwila (*Intsia bijuga*, also known as Merbau) or Solomon Island beech (*Nothofagus*).

ETHYL ALCOHOL
Ethyl alcohol is the solvent for SHELLAC. In its purist form, it is generally not available for sale to the public, for it is commonly subject to an excise tax and is the basis of alcoholic beverages. It is usually rendered impure by addition of other liquids that "denature" it and render it undrinkable. Ethyl alcohol is hygroscopic and will attract water when exposed to the air. When used for dissolving shellac, it should be noted that this moisture may turn the shellac slightly cloudy. If this becomes a problem, it may be necessary to obtain a permit to purchase anhydrous alcohol. Methylated spirit is a common variety of denatured alcohol, and is the same as the U.S. government-approved product.

EXPLODED VIEW
See E–11.
Drawings of carvings that are built up from components are often set out in an "exploded" form, so that the individual pieces can be clearly seen, while at the same time their location in the finished form is clear. The OVERLAY is another way of achieving a similar result.

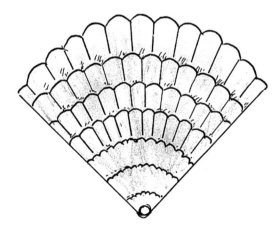

E–09
The scallop shell has formed the basis of much symbolism throughout history, and has adorned or been a part of many things from the humble mirror crest to the almighty corporate logo.

E–11
This drawing is part of the exploded view of drawings for the carving that decorates the inside of the lid of the chisel chest seen in illustration C–13.

EXCULPTATE

To exculptate means "to carve out," and is derived from the Latin *exculptus*. The origins of the term SCULPTURE are obvious!

FACE

The face of a piece of timber is usually the largest surface area, the EDGE being the smallest, other than the end. The face of a GRINDING WHEEL is also its largest surface area, the edge normally being the surface that faces the operator, and the face of a woodcarving gouge is normally the cutting edge.

FERRULE

See F–01.

A ferrule is a metal band or ring on the woodcarving tool that helps prevent the handle splitting or the wood of the handle generally moving.

It helps to ensure the blade remains firmly housed in the handle. Ferrules on woodcarving chisels may be internal or external. The internal ferrule is hidden from view and is forced into the end of the handle where the hole for the TANG commences. The external ferrule is a band over the wood at the end of the handle that rests against the stop on the tang.

FILAMENT LIGHTING

See F–02.

"Filament" lights make the best form of artificial lighting for woodcarving as they produce light rays that cause the creation of strong shadows when positioned to form CROSS LIGHT. The regular household light bulb is a filament light. HALOGEN lights are similar. "Neon," or "FLUORESCENT" tubes, which generally produce diffused light, are not recommended for woodcarving. Lights will vary in intensity, width of beam, and color. Color in normal domestic lights may vary from a yellow tinge, to bluish tinge, to bright white, depending on their COLOR TEMPERATURE. Some experimentation may be needed to ascertain the most favorable for the individual;

F–01

The handle on the left of this illustration has an internal ferrule pressed into its end. The handle in the middle has an external ferrule. The handle on the right is made from a small branch of a tree, and is fitted into the conical cup of the blade on the far right. This is the kind of tool that is in common usage in Thailand and other Asian countries.

F-02
A light bulb with a tungsten filament is best for woodcarving, as it creates good shadows.

however, the white light of tungsten halogen lights is probably the most suitable.

FILE

A file is made from hardened steel and has fine teeth cut into it. Files are manufactured in a wide variety of sizes and shapes, and are used mostly for metal work. They can be used for smoothing wood, particularly where some texture may be required in awkward places. A round CROSS SECTION "rat tail" file is useful for cleaning around holes in PIERCED RELIEF, and a "triangle" file is useful for corners. A RIFFLER FILE and a RASP are specifically made for woodcarving.

FILLER

A filler is generally one of two things in woodwork. First, it may be an inert pigment in the form of a finely powdered substance that is mostly used as a "cheapener" for formulations, or to alter the structural properties of a substance. Second, and more commonly, it describes a substance used for repair work. In this context, there are a number of characteristics to consider:
✔ The material may shrink, even to the extent that it falls out.
✔ It may "age" to a different color from the wood being repaired.
✔ It may have a different surface texture that will make it visible.
✔ It may not accept the surface finish intended for the carving.
   Given these potential shortcomings, it is essential to test the "filler" on a wood scrap or unseen part of the carving before completing the repair.

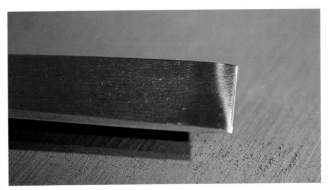

F-03
The straight chisel is to be used with caution, for the corners may dig in and create "tram tracks" on the surface of the wood.

FIRMER

See F-03.
A firmer chisel is a general-purpose chisel that can be used with a mallet. It is the common carpenter's chisel. In woodcarving, the term is sometimes interchanged with the carver's STRAIGHT CHISEL. The firmer chisel may be used as a substitute for the carver's straight chisel for convex work (a SKEW is a better choice) and for cleaning edges and undercutting.

FISHTAIL

See F-04.
A fishtail tool is so called because of the shape of its blade. These gouges or straight chisels are generally used for finishing work where a MALLET is not required and delicate handwork is appropriate. They are also very useful for lettering to access fine corners, and for the shaping of serifs. They are generally light to the touch in the hand and predispose the user to lighter cutting than a straight-sided GOUGE.

F-04
Prepare the fishtail with a long, thin bevel, and it will be an excellent tool for fine finishing.

FLAKING

Flaking is a characteristic of wood that is not present in all species, but when it is it can cause considerable "trouble" for the inexperienced carver. The wood literally flakes off. If this occurs, try approaching the wood from a different direction, or making a shallower cut. Sometimes it occurs because the wood is too dry, and this can be relieved by application of a fine mist of water from an atomizer. To be successful the tool must be very finely honed and the bevel not too thick in cross section. The thinner and finer the edge of the tool, the better. Flaking is another expression for tearing, where this occurs not so much as a rough, furry surface but more a layered TEARING CUT.

FLAT BEVEL

See F–05.
A flat bevel is the easiest to grind on to a woodcarving tool. It is achieved by using the flat FACE of a wheel and not the circumference or edge, which will hollow-grind the tool. Unlike a CON-

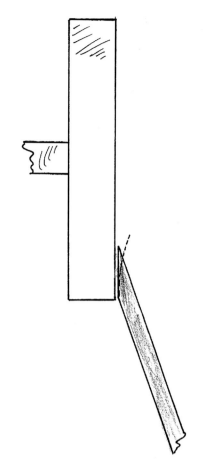

F–05
Be sure to keep the tool cool by dipping in a tin of water during the grinding process. Experiment with slightly convex bevels, as they may be easier to use than flat bevels.

CAVE BEVEL or a CONVEX BEVEL, a flat bevel is "neutral" and will neither push the tool out of the wood nor help stop it from nose-diving into the wood. A flat bevel may be a disadvantage, as nearly all carving actions require the tool to come up and out of the wood. A very slight convex bevel is best.

FLATNESS

Unless a carved surface is meant to be flat, flatness is the curse of the carver—like straight lines that are crooked and circles that aren't. Most often it is the convex curve that isn't convex enough. We tend to leave a flat spot on the tops of beads or berries, or people's faces are too

flat with the corners of the eyes not pulled back far enough, or the forehead not curved enough.

Note that the illusion of a round surface can be achieved by combining the effect of an almost flat top (on a bead or berry, for instance) with a tightly curved edge around the perimeter. Apply cross lighting, and "flat" can look "round."

In nature subjects, it is important to remember there are no flat surfaces. So if there is a flat spot on the carving, chances are it should not be there.

FLUORESCENT LIGHTING

Fluorescent light is unsuitable as a specific light for woodcarving because it doesn't allow for the creation of shadows. Fluorescent tubes nevertheless may be suitable for general ambient lighting. Different light types produce different-colored light because of their COLOR TEMPERATURE. It is important that if fluorescent overhead lights for ambient light are to be mixed with other kinds of light that create cross lighting,

F–06
Fluters are excellent tools for creating fancy scroll work, and they are a good choice for creating fabric folds on carvings in the round.

FLUTERONI

See F–07.

A fluteroni, unlike the MACARONI, has curved corners and is for finishing sides of recesses. It is generally a straight gouge; however, some older tools are SHORT BENT and LONG BENT. Fluteronis are not frequently used, and are therefore a specialist tool. They may be used for specific traditional design such as an acanthus leaf pattern. The sharpening technique for these tools is similar to the "V" tool. A fluteroni with a ridged or raised bottom is called a backeroni.

FOCAL LINE

See F–08.

A focal line is a prominent line, ridge, division

F–07
This fluteroni is handy for hollowing out contours such as leaf shapes; however, it is not a common tool purchase. A gouge is a reasonable substitute, although a fluteroni will often give a faster result.

they both be of compatible color temperature, otherwise the mix of color might be too irritating for the carver.
A good combination is "daylight" fluorescent general lighting above the workspace, and tungsten halogen cross lighting.

FLUTER

See F–06.

A fluter is similar to a GOUGE, but with higher sides. A high-sided fluter is a VEINER. A fluter is used for creating shallow recesses. SHARPENING the fluter must be done with great care, particularly on a GRINDING WHEEL, as it is very

easy overheat the thin sides of the tool or grind them away without realizing until it is too late. It is not appropriate to use a mallet with a small thin-walled fluter, as it may bend.

F–08
With the position of the focal line correctly identified, the other parts of the buffalo can be accurately located.

or other extended part of a design that is an area of focal attention to the eye. It is to be distinguished from a FOCAL POINT. The focal line in F–08 is the ridge along the top of the water buffalo. It is important to identify focal lines before the carving commences because they become those parts of the carving that draw attention. They are the parts of the carving from which, and to which, the other parts of the design flow. If they are in the wrong place or they are the wrong shape, they will throw everything else out of place, and distort and potentially ruin the overall effect of the carving.

F–09
Focal points as indicated by the red arrowheads must be correctly located for the buffalo to take on the right proportions.

accentuating natural features can make some amazing art. It is important to clean "found wood" before carving commences to remove sand and dirt that might damage tools. Hose the lump of wood down, and brush or vacuum it. Start by removing bark (that will probably fall off) and see what can be found underneath!

FRAMES

Careful selection of timber for frames and BORDERS is important. If they are to hang on a wall, weight is a major

FOCAL POINT

See F–09.

A focal point is similar to a FOCAL LINE and it is the part of the design that is prominent and key to the positioning of the less prominent parts of the design. It is very important that focal points be identified and correctly located in the carving before the other elements of the design are carved. In F–09, there are five focal points indicated by red arrowheads. The tip of the nose, the tips of the horns, the rise in the

spine before the tail, and the beginning of the tail are all focal points. If these are in the wrong place, the buffalo cannot be properly constructed.

FOUND WOOD SCULPTURE

See F–10.

This piece of cherry fruit wood is a pruning from a domestic garden tree. Conceptually, this style of work takes a lump of wood found in the garden, bush, or forest, and the artist sees what can be made of it. Searching for color and shape and

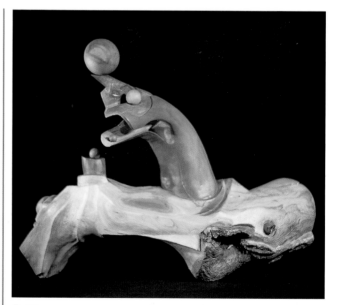

F–10
The artist called this found wood sculpture "The Magic Dragon." There is a dragon in there somewhere, and the round balls decorating it can be moved around in a modular fashion to alter its appearance.

consideration. The weight of the mirror or a painting and its protective glass must be taken into consideration. Usually lightweight softwoods are used, such as pines, jelutong (*Dyera costulata*), or lime. Ensure the wood for the frame is seasoned before assembly, otherwise WARP may occur.

FRENCH CURVES

See F–11.
The curved TEMPLATES in this set are known as French curves. There is a wide range of French curve templates, each set offering an endless variety of curves for many drawing applications. These are particularly useful for developing designs and patterns. They are not used frequently; however, they do allow the carver who does not have a skilled drawing hand to easily create original material. French curves can be purchased from art and drawing supply retailers.

FRETSAW

See F–12.
A fretsaw is a frame saw with a very fine blade that can be used for cutting veneer and inlay. For woodcarving, it would be used mainly for piercing through wood to create PIERCED RELIEF. However, it is more likely that a heavier-duty style of saw would be used, like a COPING SAW. The blade for a fretsaw is generally clamped in

F–12
Fretsaws can be awkward to use. Make sure the blade is well tensioned, and have a good, well-controlled hand grip. For most carving situations a coping saw or scroll saw would be an easier choice.

F–11
French curves help to create smooth curves and attractive shapes.

place whereas a coping saw blade is tensioned and held in place by a flexible frame pushing against a pin at each end of the blade. This system makes it much easier to remove and to re-install the blade constantly, as is necessary with the piercing of relief carving.

FRONT BENT

A front bent gouge is the same as the SPOON BIT GOUGE.

F–13
Before re-using timber from old dusty furniture, scrub it down to remove dirt and mold. Washing will not damage old wood so long as it does not remain wet. When removing bark from logs, be sure no dirt or mold growth is breathed in.

FUNGUS
See F–13.
There are many types of fungus or mold that may be present in both new and used (recycled) wood. It is important to wear a face mask or respirator when band sawing and cleaning timber. Fungus also discolors and may cause wood to rot, so it is important to store wood in a dry place and off the ground to reduce the chances of the transfer of fungal spores. Some species of wood are rot resistant, so if a garden sculpture is considered, select one that has the prospects of a good outdoor life.

GADROON
A gadroon is a style of decoration used on the edges of furniture, similar to NULLING.

GARNET PAPER
See G–01.
Garnet is a hard, glass-like silicate mineral. There are a variety of colors and the one commonly used as an ABRASIVE for timber is orange. It is adhered to a cloth or paper backing. Another common abrasive ideal for timber is ALUMINUM OXIDE. Some abrasives are more suitable than others for wood, and because abrasives vary considerably, some experimentation is necessary. "Blunt" or worn sanding paper will not cut efficiently or cleanly, and all sanding papers will "round off" sharp edges unless they are used with great care.

G CLAMP
See G–02.
Like CRAMPS, one of the most common and useful clamps can also be a source of danger for the woodcarver. Not from the user safety point of view, but from the point of view of the safety of the carving itself. Here are some points to watch for:
✔ Always place a scrap of thin wood between the face of the jaw of the clamp and the carving so as not to bruise the carving.
✔ If for any reason the carving is not flat, never place a clamp on opposite corners without supporting the edge that is raised off the surface by the curve in the wood, otherwise the pressure from the clamps will CRACK the carving.
✔ Always ensure the clamps are applying pressure in a direction that will not break or crack a protruding part like an arm or a leg or a

G–01
Garnet paper is excellent for sanding raw wood. Make sure the paper being used is not clogged with wood dust, and wear a dust mask or respirator.

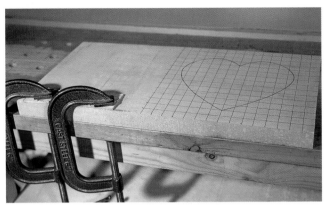

G–02
Place "G clamps" in a position that will not interfere with the carving activity or damage tools.

leaf. Wherever possible clamp on the main body.
✔ Whenever possible, place the clamp on the bench so that the handle and excess thread are below the bench, not pointing upwards above it, where it may cause eye or face damage by accidentally leaning into it.

GESSO

See G–03 and G–04.
Gesso is a mixture of rabbit-skin glue, distilled water, and chalk whiting, applied as a thin paste. It is the coating that is applied to surfaces before they are gilded. Gesso forms a porous underlay that can be sanded to a very smooth finish before the application of oil or WATER GILDING. For the carver, if a decoration is to be gessoed, it is very important to carve the work in such a way that allowance is made for the thickness of the coating, so that after it is applied, the decoration is still visible. There will probably be additional coatings of clay or bole in the case of gilding, each adding to the thickness of the layer on the timber. The carving may require deeper cutting in parts to ac-

G–03
A gilder will add a thick layer of gesso over the timber surface. Gesso is often stored in airtight containers and applied with a brush.

G–04
If a carving is to be gilded, discuss its carving with the gilder before completing it. Some detail work may not be appropriate for the addition of gold leaf, which may, in addition to gesso, have a layer of yellow bole beneath it.

commodate this coating. Generally gilding is not successfully completed over sharp edges because the gold leaf fractures; so these should also be avoided in the carving process. The gilding process may add up to $\frac{1}{32}$ inch layer on to the wood.

GESSO HOOK

See G–05.
The GESSO hook is used to scrape away excess gesso from the surface of the carving before gilding commences. It is used as a SCRAPER for trimming and shaping before final sanding. The face of the tool should be ground flat, and while the tool does not need

to be razor sharp, it should nevertheless be able to scrape the surface cleanly without scratching the soft chalk. The tool should be wiped clean after use to reduce the likelihood of rusting, especially if the chalk is not quite dry.

GLANCING BLOW

See G–06.
While using a MALLET, ensure the correct mallet shape and weight is used, and that it is held correctly. Incorrect shape and POSTURE are both causes of making glancing blows that may cause damage to the carving. It is of great importance that the carver be comfortable, and that

G–06
A round mallet helps prevent glancing blows; however, posture is very important for tool control.

once the correct tools are being used, they are used in such a way that discomfort does not cause error and subsequent frustration. Be sure the posture is not cramped and awkward, and that the chisel is held firmly so that a mallet blow will not dislodge it.

GLASS PAPER

Ground glass has been used for "sandpaper" in the past, and whereas it is not generally seen in modern economies, the term lingers. More common ABRASIVES are made from ALUMINUM OXIDE and SILICON CARBIDE.

GLUE

A correct choice of glue for repair work or LAMINATING blocks or panels requires thought:
✔ The glue must be suitable for the timber. Greasy or oily wood may require washing with alcohol or acetone.
✔ The glue must be able to sustain any mechanical stresses placed on it.
✔ The color of the glue when dry must be compatible with the desired appearance of the carving.
✔ It should be "carvable" at least to the extent that it will not shatter under a chisel cut.
✔ It should not be so

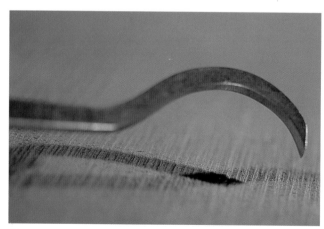

G–05
Some manufacturers still include a gesso hook in their "sets" of tools, although the majority of people would never use it for this purpose. It can also be used as a scraper for cleaning up awkward and hard-to-reach places.

"thick" that it prevents a repair from seating to its original position.

✔ It must not be so hard that it will damage the fine edge of a chisel. Glue products vary significantly market to market, so specific recommendations will not be made. However, as a guide, isocyanate glues are suitable for instant repair of small parts. They will shatter under pressure, so use only where there is no need for further carving. PVA (polyvinyl acetate) glues are generally suitable where further carving is required. Resin glues may set very hard and may not be suitable.

GLUING UP

A new break should be repaired immediately, before the individual fibers and CELLS in the grain become displaced and will not go back to their original positions. If you are preparing blocks or panels, apart from ensuring you read the manufacturer's instructions and act accordingly, be aware that if you follow "normal" woodwork practice of alternating grain direction to improve stability, you may

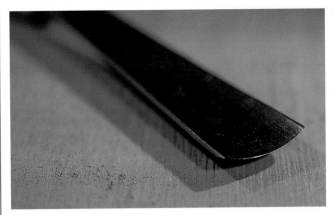

G–07
A gouge is the woodcarver's primary tool. Select it carefully—choosing a well-balanced range to reduce expense and avoid confusion on the workbench.

well be making your carving activity harder. This is not to say don't do it, but to just be aware of it.

GOUGE

See G–07.
A gouge has a hollow (concave) cross section for cutting curves. In woodcarving, the gouge is commonly referred to as a CHISEL. There are many, many shapes and sizes of gouge, many specialist designs for use in particular trades such as cooperage, pattern making, and coach building. The woodcarver alone is faced with choices of many hundreds of gouge shapes. For the new woodcarver, the most

effective way to approach these choices is to carefully select tools one a time, as and when they are needed. As experience grows, fewer and fewer tools will be needed for the average kind of work most people will do, so there is a danger that too many unnecessary tools will be purchased when just starting out.

GRAIN

See AGAINST THE GRAIN.
"Grain" is a generic term for the combination of cells and fibers that make up wood.

GRID LINES

See G–08.
"Grid lines" make a very useful method for enlarging, reducing, or transferring designs, without the need for calculators or photocopiers or computers or a PANTOGRAPH! The "grid line method" al-

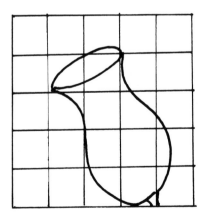

G–08
Ensure the grid lines are accurately spaced, and choose a scale that is convenient. Whole-number multiples are easy to estimate by eye. This scale is 2:1, or twice the size of the original seed.

lows scaling of the drawing simply by converting the size of the grid squares to larger or smaller depending on the objective. In the illustration, the pattern is being enlarged, before being transferred to the wood with CARBONIZED PAPER. Care needs to be taken estimating the distances within each square. If the grid is large, it may be necessary to subdivide the square to make it easier to use. Prepared "graph paper" makes the process even easier to use accurately.

GRINDING WHEEL

See G–09, G–10, G–11 and G–12.

The "bench grinder" is a favorite for repairing, reshaping, and sharpening all kinds of tools, including those for woodcarving. Bench grinders generally run at a speed of around 1400 revolutions per minute, and the main variables are the diameter and construction of the wheel. A WATER WHEEL is a variation of the bench grinder.

The majority of grinding wheels are made from gray silicon carbide or white aluminum

G–10
If the grinding wheel is as coarse as this one, it is not suitable for fine grinding of woodcarving tools. This wheel is made from gray silicon carbide.

oxide. Aluminum oxide is often preferred for tool grinding, because it absorbs heat quickly and transfers it away from the cutting surface, thereby tending to keep the tool edge cooler, which in turn helps maintain the "temper" (hardness) of the tool steel.

In many cases, however, it is not the material of the wheel that matters, but the coarseness or fineness of the cutting surface of the wheel. This will be the result of two factors, first the size of the "grit" or "grain" of the abrasive, and the manner in which it is bonded together. If it is a coarse grain bonded together in an open manner, the wheel will be fairly

G–09
The best grinding machines have well-balanced bearings and shaft, and do not vibrate. If there is vibration, check that the wheel itself is correctly and firmly centered on the spindle, and is mounted exactly at right angles to it.

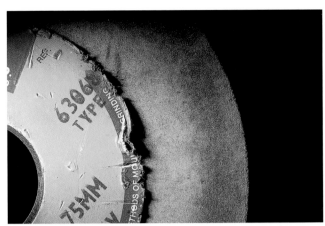

G–11
This wheel has an acceptable "coarseness" for grinding woodcarving tools. The wheel is made from white aluminum oxide.

rough. If it a fine grain and bonded very closely and "tightly," it will be a very fine wheel. Openly bonded and coarse grains burn tool steel less than closely bonded fine grains, but the latter produce a far smoother tool surface, which needs less work to create a polished surface. The best for woodcarving tools is a "120 grain" (very fine) aluminum oxide wheel very closely bonded. This will produce a very clean surface on the tool, but will also burn the tool easily if care is not taken. Grinding wheels require frequent dressing with a DIAMOND STICK to maintain a keen cutting (grinding) surface.

GROOVE

See G–13.
"Making a groove" is a common expression in the language of the carver. It might be for decorating feathers, or to represent veins on a leaf or mortar between bricks on a wall. Whatever the intention, one of the most common ways to try to make the "groove" is with the PARTING TOOL. Unfortunately, this is not always the best way. It is vital to experiment first on a scrap of wood, before unnecessary damage is created. The "V" tool is often not a "V" at all, but a finely rounded "U" and can ruin the artist's intended impression. The heel of the SKEW chisel, or a KNIFE, may be the best way to create the intended "groove," cutting each side independently.

G–12
This is the same wheel as in illustration G–11; however, it is now clogged with debris from grinding tools, and must be cleaned by dressing the surface with a diamond stick, otherwise it will burn the chisels.

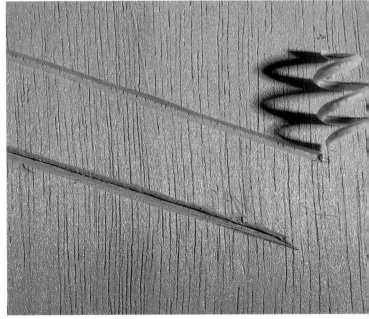

G–13
The groove at the top of the illustration was made with a "V" tool, and the one at the bottom with two cuts from a knife.

G–14
The groundwork in this carving is flawed by poor cutting of wavy and interlocked grain. The uneven surface is unfortunately reflecting considerable light in a ring around the problem area below the scroll. The carving is from a card design included in Thomas Murner's "Chartiludium Institute Summarie," Strasbourg, 1518.

GROUND

The "ground" is the background in a relief carving. It is not necessarily the background of the actual design (for example, the clouds or hills "in the background") but it is the surface of the remaining timber. The process of establishing the parameters of the background is sometimes known as "grounding in."

GROUNDWORK

See G–14.
Groundwork has the actual pattern or "relief" rising from it. Groundwork is the act of creating the ground, and the resulting appearance of it. It may, for example, be smooth, textured by a PUNCH, flat, or sloping. Groundwork is an integral part of the carving, and therefore is just as important as the remainder. In this respect, it is imperative that as much attention to its finish be applied as to the remainder of the carving. Backgrounds that are cut by chisel marks, torn by poor techniques, uneven in depth, lumpy, or rising up to the pattern instead of being cleanly delineated from it by UNDERCUTTING are examples of the most common errors.

GROWTH RING

See G–15.
The growth rings in wood represent different layers of growth that correspond to growing seasons. Their size will depend on things such as weather conditions and the shape and arrangement of CELLS. Their color may depend on such things as whether they are from active or inactive cells, as in HEARTWOOD and sapwood, and whether they are early or late growth during a season. Growth rings affect the direction in which wood may WARP, and they will dictate GRAIN direction.

GUM TURPENTINE

Gum turpentine is distilled from the sap of pine trees and is a colorless liquid with an agreeable RESIN odor. It is a volatile and slightly toxic solvent, used in commercial paint and VARNISH, and is a solvent for beeswax in high-quality furniture polishes. It evaporates slowly, so it is convenient for applications where "time" is needed, such as the application of polish or brushing varnish. It is also used as a solvent in artist's paints. It is not to be confused with mineral turpentine, a petroleum distillate also used as a thinner for commercial paints and varnishes.

HACK

Hacking, which is chopping or roughly cutting, is a poor carving technique. Skills should be developed so that rough

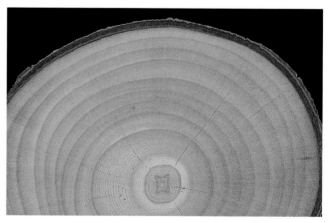

G–15
The growth rings in this piece of Jacaranda are clearly visible. Visibility will vary from species to species.

work is not an outcome, unless it is used for deliberate effect. It will normally by caused by one or more of poor POSTURE, BLUNTNESS of tools, inappropriate-shaped tools (particularly the BEVEL), or inappropriate selection of timber for the pattern. Carving AGAINST THE GRAIN is also a very common cause of a hacked appearance. A well-controlled, sharp tool skillfully passed through the wood in the "right" direction will avoid these troubles. The best way to achieve this equilibrium is experimentation.

HACK HAMMER

A hack hammer is a tool like an ADZE, with a hammerhead, used for dressing stone. It is clearly not a woodworking tool. However, in some cases, tools used in other crafts may well be appropriate for woodcarving. Some examples are: A carpenters chisel can be used as a substitute for a firmer chisel in carving; leather punches may be used as background punches for wood; some metal engraving tools can be used for wood; the coni-

H–01
Illustrated is the hacksaw, used for cutting metal. A woodcarver will probably only ever use it for cutting a ferrule. It may be necessary to ream off the burred edge of the ferrule with a rattail file before fitting.

cal polyurethane bush from a truck suspension system makes a great carver's mallet head; dentist's probes can be used for cleaning up in tight corners; and a violin maker's plane might be used for fine scraping. The moral here is simply: keep an open mind, and experiment!

HACKSAW

See H–01 and H–02.
A hacksaw is a framed saw with a blade specifically designed for cutting metal. Its only relevance to woodcarving is that the blade is sometimes useful for texturing a surface. The blade is not appropriate

for cutting wood. Woodcarving is an art form, and as is often the case the creation of desired visual effects is not always possible with the "standard" tools that are available for the craft;

improvisation, as with a HACKHAMMER, is sometimes a necessity. The hacksaw blade has very fine teeth that are very close together and can be used to "rough up" a surface or make

H–02
Texture effects like this can be achieved with a hacksaw blade. Experimentation with different tools from other disciplines will add considerable flexibility to the carver's skills.

shallow scratches. It will create a "WOOLLY" surface that might be useful for the center of a flower or to represent fur on an animal.

HALOGEN LIGHT

See H–03.

Halogen lighting is a very effective means of creating CROSS LIGHTING to carve by. It produces a very white light and its physical size makes it a convenient modern lighting alternative. The majority of domestic halogen lights are 12 volts and the fittings have built-in transform-

H–03
Halogen lighting is economical, creates white light, and the width of the beam can be varied by using different bulbs. It gets quite hot, so be careful of burns.

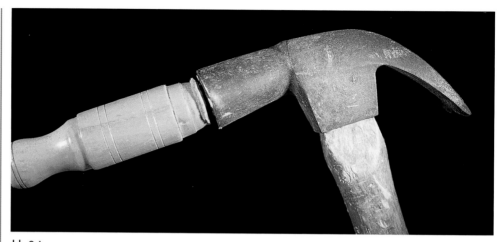

H–04
Builder's hammers are definitely not for woodcarving. A shaped and balanced carver's mallet that will not destroy tool handles is essential for successful carving.

ers. Halogen light bulbs are available with different widths of light beam, often varying anywhere from 5 degrees to 60 degrees or more, so a controlled light environment is possible. Generalized lighting such as that from a FLUORESCENT light is not appropriate for woodcarving, where shadows need to be created.

HAMMER

See H–04.

The modern hammer has a metal head, is manufactured in a variety of configurations for a variety of purposes, and is entirely unsuitable as a woodcarving MALLET. Metal heads will destroy wooden carving

chisel handles, and the design and shape of a metal hammerhead has the wrong balance and is the wrong size for use with woodcarving tools. The small size of the flat head will cause the hammer to slide off the carving tool's handle, and may injure the hand holding the chisel.

HAND STRENGTH

Woodcarving is an activity that will develop the strength of the hands over time. If it is a new activity, at first there may be some muscle soreness in the fingers and forearm after prolonged work. The use of a MALLET that is too heavy or too light may also cause muscular problems,

which in the longer term may be diagnosed as "repetitive strain injury." It should not be necessary to undertake any hand strengthening exercises; however, if it is necessary, try repetitive squeezing of a small rubber ball between the thumb and fingers. If there is any doubt, or ARTHRITIS is a problem, seek medical advice.

HANDLE

See H–05 and H–06.

The handle of any tool is of great importance. Comfort to the user is the most significant factor, and there are as many handle designs as there are tools. Some traditional carving chisel handle shapes are

H–05
A comfortable handle is important for the woodcarver, and essential for fine control.

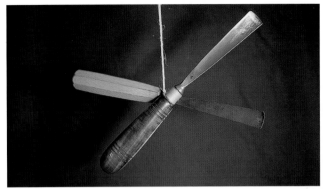

H–06
The heavier handle in this illustration is made from Australian gidgee (*Acacia cambegei*), weighing in at 88 lbs per ft³ (1330 Kg per m³).

shown in the illustrations. Just as shape is important, so is the material the handle is made from. If it is wood, it must be from a species that has high end-grain impact strength to take constant blows from a mallet. Woods such as European beech, and Canadian rock maple have high end-grain impact strength. Dense woods like the one used in H–06 that make a handle heavier than the blade are ideal, because the balance of the tool is hand heavy and this gives the carver greater control.

HANDLE REPLACEMENT

See H–07.
At some stage every carver will have to replace a broken chisel handle. The vast majority of modern tools are made to

a configuration that has a tang on the end of the blade which fits up into the handle, and an internal or external FERRULE. When fitting a new handle, ensure the hole that the blade fits up into is the right size, otherwise the handle will split as the tang is forced into it. Ideally a TAPERED bit is used to create the hole.

If this is not available, bore at least two different-diameter holes to create a similar effect. Usually, the last ¼ inch of the of the pointed tang will be forced into the wood at the bottom of the hole, so make the hole that much shorter. If the hole ends up being too large, it will be necessary to anchor the blade with glue.

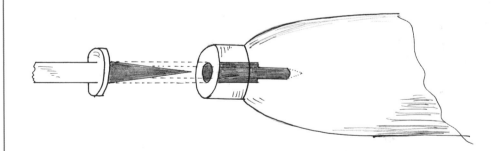

H–07
Great care must be taken when preparing to fit a new handle. It is very easy to split the handle if the hole that accepts the tang is too small. If there is any doubt, experiment with different drill sizes in scrap timber.

HARMONIOUS

Harmony for the wood-carver is a design aesthetic. The design characteristics of content, balance, and perspective create the COMPOSITION and therefore they all play a part in the harmony of the creation. Like or dislike is generally in the eye of the beholder, so it is very difficult to lay down rules about harmonious composition. The most common errors causing disharmony are:

✔ Incorrect proportion—the eyes in the wrong place on a head, the body too large

✔ Flat surfaces that should be curved. Generally in nature, subjects in relief or in the round have no flat surfaces

✔ Scrolls or other curves that do not flow—a scroll should flow evenly along the complete curve; interruptions to the even flow of a curve will be very obvious as humps or bumps and should be trimmed off

✔ Incorrect perspective—perspective for relief carving is difficult to achieve, and is learned as a technique of shadow creation; shadows are used to create illusions of depth and distance

HATCHET

See H–08.
A hatchet is a light ax, and is useful for a carver of SCULPTURE or other work in the round. The hatchet is used for shaping in a limited way, and is also useful for the

H–09
The adornment with carving of entranceways and windows has long disappeared. However, some modern homes now have head-light windows as a decorative feature. Could the head mold ever make a comeback?

H–08
A hatchet is an ideal tool for rough shaping and for removing bark. Be careful using a hatchet when you are bending over as it is easy to strike a glancing blow and cut into your leg.

clearing of bark from logs. Tools such as these do not have many applications in the creation process itself; however, together with a bush saw and an ADZE the hatchet is more a wood-gathering and -preparation tool.

HEAD MOLD

See H–09.
The head mold is an architectural item. It is the molding projecting over the head of a window or door. In past times it was often decorated with carving.

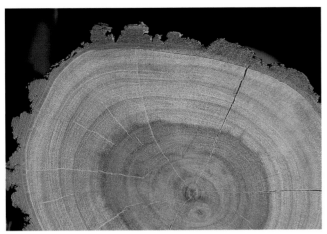

H–10
In this piece of myall (*Acacia glaucescens*), the heartwood is clearly distinguishable from the sapwood. In some species, this is not the case, and the two are sometimes indistinguishable to the naked eye.

HEARTWOOD
See H–10.
Heartwood is that group of the CELLS of the tree that make up the GROWTH RINGS which are no longer required for the transporting of nutrients. These are the cells closest to the center of the tree and are characteristically darker in color than the remainder of the tree, which is mostly the SAPWOOD that is characteristically lighter in color. It is the heartwood that gives the tree wood the color and GRAIN figure for which it is recognized. So the dark red-brown of mahogany, for example, is the color of the heartwood. Heartwood is normally the preferred part of the tree for carving, as it is denser, more uniform, and more predictable in its behavior with tools than is sapwood.

HIGH RELIEF
Different kinds of RELIEF CARVING defined by the depth of the carving.

HOLDFAST
See H–11.
This style of holding device is particularly useful for holding smaller carvings in the round, and panels for relief carving. It requires boring a hole in the BENCHTOP, and it has a disadvantage in that unless there are alternative holes bored, it remains always in the same place. Care must be taken not to damage the chisel end on the metal shaft or plate of the holdfast, and it may be necessary to place a thin piece of wood under the holding plate to prevent damage to the surface of the carving.

HOLLOW GRINDING
Hollow grinding is the making of a CONCAVE BEVEL on the carving tool. A concave BEVEL is inappropriate for carving tools, as this shape will encourage the tool to nosedive into the surface of the wood. Hollow grinding is achieved by grinding the tool on the circumference or edge of a GRINDING WHEEL,

H–11
If there is the slightest unevenness in the panel being carved, anchoring it at a corner like this will raise the other corner, which must be packed to avoid instability on the bench and probable cracking.

H–12

Specialist restoration work is a potential source of employment for the keen woodcarver. Searching out such activity can take a woodcarver to some amazing places.

HOOD MOLDING

See H–12.

In architecture, the hood molding is the upper projecting molding above the arch of a Gothic window. These sometimes extraordinarily complex carvings are not generally produced in modern times, unless for restoration work. It is for this reason—which is the ability to conduct restoration work—that the skills of woodcarving must not be lost in the future.

and it is the method used for shaping spindle gouges for wood turning on a lathe. A convex bevel is used for bowl gouges. The degree of hollow grind or concave curve will be governed by the diameter of the grinding wheel.

HONING

Honing is the activity of stropping for a finely polished surface. There are three stages to preparing a tool for use. First, there is using a GRINDING WHEEL to establish the basic shape of the tool, then SHARP-ENING generally on a stone (natural or synthetic) to establish a sharp edge, and last, honing to a scratch-free polished edge using a STROP. Honing may be done on leather, which is the most common method, and various abrasives may be added to the surface of the leather to enhance the process and make it faster. Honing is extremely important, as it is this activity that creates the "razor edge" needed for fine carving.

I–01

Undercutting on round surfaces, or in difficult-to-get-at places, may require the use of reverse bent or back bent gouges, which were used to undercut these imbricated leaves.

IMBRICATE

See I–01.

To imbricate in wood-carving is to make something appear to overlap. In the illustration the leaves are carved to give the impression that each one overlaps another. This design style relies on the creation of SHADOWS by deep undercutting. The choice of timber is important if this is to be undertaken successfully. The example uses Brazilian mahogany, which is relatively easy to carve and dense enough to hold together with large amounts of undercut area. Woods that CHIP or break or are otherwise unstable must be avoided. These are generally those with coarse open grain.

IMPOST

See I–02.

In architecture, the impost is the place where an arch rests on a wall or column. The impost is usually marked with horizontal moldings. It

I–02
If there is a desire to carve architectural components for the home or other building, make sure the dimensions of the wood, after carving, remain sufficiently strong to do the intended job. Carving over joints is equally problematical. This impost is about 18 inches (457mm) wide.

I–03
Incised lettering such as this requires accurate setting out of the letter patterns (the "font"); clean, well-executed cuts will ensure a smart appearance.

is conceivable that the modern home with a so-called "cathedral ceiling" could also incorporate imposts with some imaginative architectural designing.

INCISED

See I–03.

In woodcarving, incised means "cut in," similar to engraving. It is a commonly used style for lettering, called "incised lettering." The opposite is "raised lettering." CHIP CARVING is also incised, as is a WOODCUT for printing. Incising is not done with any particular tool, although some shapes are easier to use, such as a FIRMER chisel, a SKEW chisel, or a SPADE gouge.

65

INTAGLIO

See I–04 and I–05.
Carving or engraving below the surface or cutting a die that can be used to press a relief design (like a BUTTER MOLD) is known as "carving in intaglio." To carve in this manner requires a specially developed ability to see the design in the negative, and an estimation of the depth of cuts so that they create the correct height and shape when the impression is molded. To achieve an understanding of how to carve such molds, start with a simple design such as a shell, and don't make it too small. Make an impression of a shell in some WAX, and then create a wooden replica.

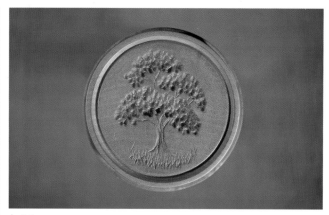

I–04
This intaglio carving is in end-grain cherry fruit wood. Imagining in reverse is all that is needed!

INTARSIA

Intarsia is the art of making a mosaic pattern by inlaying different species of wood (to achieve different colors) into the surface. The pattern is made from thin pieces laid side by side. Great accuracy is required to cut each piece so that it fits neatly beside the next. Intarsia may be used in conjunction with carving to create an overall effect, although this is not common. In the vast majority of cases intarsia is a technique used to create fancy floors.

INTERLOCKED GRAIN

See I–06.
This term refers to the CELL and fiber layout in timber. It is commonly referred to also as "wavy" grain, and it is almost impossible to cut in one direction only, such as ALONG THE GRAIN. Many harder woods are characterized by interlocked grain, and small detail is difficult to carve. The wood tends to split and break and requires great care and very finely honed tools.

I–05
This is the intaglio carving pressed into modeling wax, so that the impression is in "relief." Butter was often decorated like this.

I–06
Wavy, interlocked grain should be avoided unless it is needed for effect.

INTERNAL CHECKING

See I–07.

An internal CHECK is where there has been separation of the cells during the growth or seasoning of the wood, but it is not evident until uncovered by cutting. For the carver, this is a most unfortunate experience, particularly if care has been taken to choose the timber for its clarity. It is in these situations that the carver is faced with the philosophical need to accept things as they naturally are, or forever face rejection.

INTERNATIONAL STYLES

See I–08 to I–14.

As with all other art forms, woodcarving has styles that are identifiable as typically regional, and typical of different historical periods. Those illustrated are each demonstrative of completely different carving styles. As the carver examines art from different countries, personal preferences will emerge, and these may well influence his or her art. It is in this way that the art of one culture is transferred to influence the art of another.

I–08
Folk art from North America.

I–09
Folk art from Bali.

I–10
A tourist souvenir from Fiji.

I–11
A classic carving from Thailand.

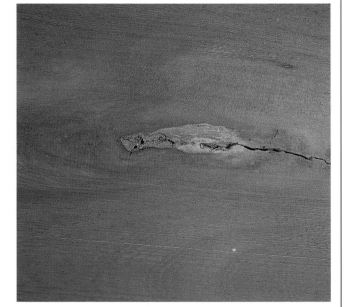

I–07
The internal check uncovered in this wood is also surrounded by rot caused by mold.

I–12
An antique carved slipper box from China.

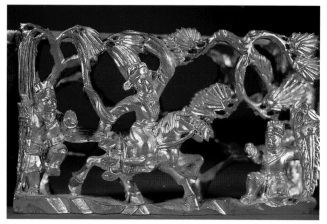

I–13
A gilded pierced relief carving also from China, showing a completely different style.

I–14
A tourist souvenir from South Africa.

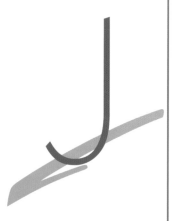

JELLY

This is a nickname for jelutong (*Dyera costulata*), a light cream-colored timber from Southeast Asia. Many timbers have different COMMON NAMES, some differing between countries and within regions of countries. Common names can be a trap for the unwary, for what is thought to be one thing might very well turn out to be completely different. There is no easy way around this, except knowledge, and wherever possible trying to identify a species by its botanical name. Unfortunately, this is not always the answer either, because botanical names are not commonly used except among the professional trades, and even these may vary. If you need to purchase timber of a particular species, a clear description, a sample, or photograph may well be the only method.

JERKY CUT

Jerky, HACK, broken, lumpy, uneven, and like terms all refer to similar outcomes of poor carving technique. The causes are several, and they each contribute to the inability to produce a smooth-sweeping cut through the timber. This is not to suggest that chisel cuts should all be long and continuous—that is most often impossible to achieve. But it does mean that the shortcuts most of us will do must flow into one another in a smooth transition that produces flowing lines and clean surfaces. You may want tool marks to remain and be visible, and this is often a desirable "hand-made" effect. It is generally better if they remain visible in a tidy and well-executed manner. Broken GRAIN, fractures, and chips are most likely undesirable effects.

JIG

See J–01.

In woodcarving a jig is a device used to guide or to hold an object. The jigs most commonly used by carvers are in the area of tool SHARPENING. Unfortunately, this is not necessarily a good thing. That is not to say that one should not use jigs for tool sharpening, but that one should be aware of their limitations. These are:

✔ Movement of the tool being sharpened is limited by the parameters of the jig. If the jig is not specifically designed for the tool, then it will impair the sharpening.

✔ If a jig is always used, the natural "free-hand skill" of the SHARPENING process will never

68

develop, or will be lost, and the carver will always rely on having a jig available. If one is not available, then sharpening will not be able to be completed satisfactorily.

✔ As a generalization, a well-developed, freehand skill allows the carver to sharpen a tool more quickly, and more accurately than with a jig.

Another kind of jig is that made for holding a carving still while it is being worked. These jigs must be robust to stop the carving from moving, and the carving should be able to be moved around for easy access.

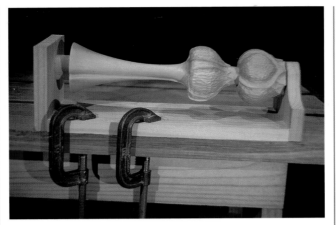

J–01
This jig for holding a turned candlestick for carving has a screw at either end that can be tightened firmly to stop the spindle turning.

J–02
Note the considerable buildup of wood dust around the blade assembly. This must be regularly cleaned away to help reduce wear on the moving parts.

JIGSAW
See J–02.
This is a particularly useful tool for the woodcarver for creating larger PIERCED RELIEF carvings (instead of using a SCROLL SAW or a COPING SAW) and trimming timber boards generally. It has depth-of-cut limitations and is not a substitute for a band saw or even a good handsaw. Regarded as a specialist tool, it is not frequently used by the average woodcarver.

JOINT
See J–03.
There are many different kinds of joint in woodwork, each designed for a different purpose, such as the DOVETAIL for chest corners. Joints, when fitted together, may or may not need either a mechanical fastener such as a nail or a screw or glue, each of which may damage woodcarving tools. Joints may also have "hidden" nails or screws as may occur in some wall paneling. For the carver, it is best to avoid carving over any joint, particularly on the corners of boxes and the like. Carving may weaken the joint, or there may be hidden nails that will damage tools, and the wood grain may vary within the joint depending on the nature of its construction, making the carving process very difficult.

JOURNEYMAN
A journeyman is a historical description of a man who was hired to work by the day. Such workers moved from

J–03
Joints such as this with internal hidden dowels should not be carved on as the carving may weaken the joint.

area to area finding work. Woodcarvers tended to work alone or in small teams of three or four, and once finished on a project would move on geographically to their next employment. Few woodcarvers ever identified their work with signature or symbol, and as they moved around, there is no way of really ever knowing who did what. A more modern meaning of journeyman is someone who has learned his trade.

JUVENILE LEAF

See J–04.
When identifying SPECIES of tree, it is sometimes beneficial to have a sample of both the juvenile leaf and the mature leaf from the species. They exhibit different characteristics, and the young leaf is often more appropriate for the botanist to use for identification purposes. Collection of leaves, bark, flowers, and seeds or nuts is a fascinating way to start to learn the identity of trees in your neighborhood. It requires the discipline of well-documented samples and the accurate recording of information, whether by photographs or sketches. A whole host of COMMON NAMES and BOTANICAL names will be discovered!

KIDSKIN

Woodcarvers often hear about using soft LEATHER such as kidskin leather for making STROPS. Kidskin leather is often used for gloves, and it is tempting to use similar soft leather for making a strop in the belief that it will be appropriate for polishing tool steel. In fact the leather is too soft, and the tool presses into it, causing the leather to roll around the edges of the tool, rounding off the sharpened edge and making it blunt. For strops, harder and thicker leather like belly hide (⅛ inch or 3mm thick) is best. Soft leather can be ideal, however, for a tool pouch or a TOOL ROLL for storing and transporting chisels.

KILN

A kiln is a heated drying chamber, and its name is derived form the Latin *culina*, meaning kitchen.

J–04
A juvenile leaf like the one at the top of this illustration has different characteristics from the mature leaf at the bottom.

For timber, the drying chamber has controlled humidity, temperature and air circulation, and is used for artificial SEASONING of wood. By gradually increasing temperature and reducing moisture the timber is "dried." Steam is often used as the heat control medium. The rate of change of temperature and humidity is important, to ensure the wood dries at a rate that will not induce CHECKING and not create a set of circumstances where the outside of the wood becomes harder and dryer than the inside. Wood typically has a moisture content of anything up to 30% when first cut from a tree. The objective of kiln drying is to reduce this moisture content to a level where the wood is stable in a normal usage environment. This is typically in the area of 10% to 14%.

KILO

In metric measurement, this is a combining measure of one thousand. A kilogram is one thousand grams. The imperial equivalent of a kilo is 2.22 pounds. When purchasing wood that has not been sawn or dressed to specific board sizes, it is often sold by weight. For example, the wood might be a block or part of a log for a sculpture. If the wood is not SEASONED, the block or log will also include a considerable amount of water, and therefore the price by weight should be considerably cheaper than the equivalent volume of timber purchased as a seasoned board. Boards are usually purchased on a lineal foot or meter basis, and the volume of wood is often expressed in SUPERFEET.

KILOWATT

A kilowatt is a measure of electrical power equivalent to a thousand watts. The typical filament household light bulb is between 60 and 100 watts. It is very important to appreciate that the higher the "wattage" of the light, the greater the amount of heat that is generated. If you are considering alternative lighting sources for your workshop, the heat generated by ten light bulbs can be considerable, particularly in the middle of summer. HALOGEN

lighting will offer a high light output for lower heat combination. FLUORESCENT lighting will offer considerably less heat than both, although being designed to be shadowless, it is not a preferred light system for woodcarving.

KINK

See K–01.
A kink is a WARP or distortion where there are stresses that arise from growth "faults" such as wavy grain or knots. Visible lengthwise along a board or strip, a kink often signifies a weakness in the timber and should be avoided for carving purposes. The wood is most likely unstable inasmuch as it may continue to move, and the wavy grain at the place of the kink will make it difficult to carve. Often these faults are not visible until the wood is

K–02
The tools shown in this illustration are all that was needed to produce the found wood sculpture in Illustration F–10, and the bust in Illustration S–07 needed only four additional tools.

cut, for it is only then that the stresses are released from the timber and it "moves" into the distorted shape.

KIT

See K–02.
The "tool kit" will be a top-of-mind subject most of the time, particularly when first starting out as a carver. It is very important not to rush

and purchase a "set" of tools predetermined by someone else. A set of chisels is also a common gift, which sometimes ends in the frustration of being given the wrong tools. Each carver is an individual, and as such will develop different techniques, objectives, and carving style from another carver. In doing so, he or she will also

K–01
Distortion, such as this kink, is often a sign of a weakness or potential further distortion, and the wood should be avoided.

develop different tool needs. What is good for one person to achieve a particular shape may well be inappropriate for another. The best advice is to purchase tools on an individual basis as and when the need arises. Tools are generally readily available, so it is relatively easy to buy them one or two at a time. Develop your tool kit as an individual, and you will not waste money or become frustrated with predetermined sets of tools—some of which you may never use.

KNOT

See K–03.
Knots are the cross section of branches that are growing out through the trunk or branch of the tree. A knot begins from the pith of the trunk or branch. Knots may be visually attractive in some cases; however, as a general rule they are not an attractive proposition for carving. In many species, the knot is tough and capable of breaking the chisel or causing serious damage. It may shrink as it dries and become loose and fall out (its grain direction is at 90 degrees to the "host" wood).

KNIFE

See K–04.
Knives are common tools for WHITTLING. There are many shapes; some are specialist tools for CHIP CARVING and the vast majority are

K–04
Select the knife for your tool kit on the basis of comfort and the shape of the blade for the application. The knife at the bottom of the illustration is a "standard" carver's knife.

general-purpose knives. It is important to use a knife in a direction away from the body and the hand holding the timber. A SKEW chisel is also a handy substitute for a knife.

KNURL

Knobs or nodules on the surface of a log indicate the presence of knots, as well as wavy and/or INTERLOCKED GRAIN below the surface. They are readily visible after the removal of the bark and are often present in clusters. If it is possible to cut them cleanly through when milling a board or making veneer, they often make an attractive feature for decorative woodwork. As for carving, they can present the same difficulty as the KNOT, and are better avoided. Unfortunately the nature of woodcarving does not often lend itself to the incorporation of wood figure in the design, unless it remains on the GROUND or in border areas.

LACQUER

See L–01.
The area of wood surface finishes is extensive, and a specialist area that needs consid-

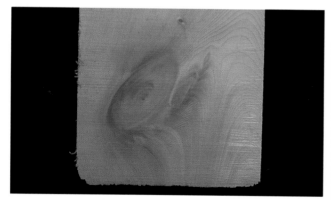

K–03
The difficulty carving a knot is increased by the likelihood that it is surrounded by wavy interlocked grain that grows around it and is compressed by it as the knot itself grows.

erable study. Some terminology that once related to specific types of finish is now generically used to cover a variety of substances, and lacquer and VARNISH are two of those words. Lacquer was generally a clear varnish consisting of SHELLAC or gum resins dissolved in alcohol. In China, which was its origin, lacquer was a resinous varnish obtained from certain trees used to give a hard, smooth, highly polished finish to wood.

L–02
Ensure that the surfaces to be glued to form a carving block are flat, and do not apply excessive and unnecessary pressure. This bracket, when carved, will house the cherub in Illustration G–04. Illustration I–01 is the part where the G clamps are, after carving.

L–01
Many carvings are spoiled by the application of a surface finish that reflects too much light from the curved surfaces, imparting a shiny plastic look. Most modern surface finishes are protective coatings designed for hard wear or weather resistance. Experiment with a proposed finish before applying it.

It is this kind of high-polish finish that should be used with some caution by the woodcarver. High gloss reflects considerable LIGHT, and the shine can interfere with the visibility of the carved detail or shape, and thus render the article unattractive.

LAMINATE
See L–02.
A common way to create a large block for SCULPTURE is to make up the required dimensions by gluing layers or boards together. This is called laminating. Where possible, the GRAIN direction should be uniform, otherwise the

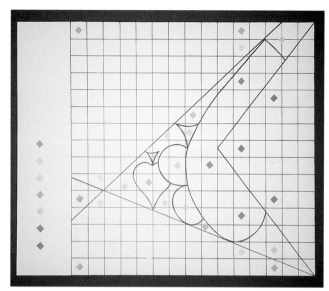

L–03
Marking the original drawing with numbers or color-coding the layers is an effective way to determine where things should be relative to one another.

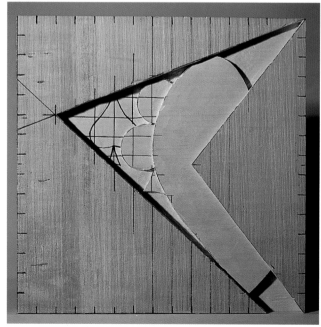

L–04
Careful planning will ensure everything will fit correctly.

design may be difficult to carve with the grain alternating direction constantly. It is also important when GLUING to choose one that will not be so hard that it may damage tools, or when dry be a stripe between the layers.

LAYERS

See L–03 and L–04.
Many carvings in relief and the round require the establishment of layers to create depth and the impression of realism. The decision making to arrive at what should be at what level in a carving can be a confusing process for the beginner. There is nothing worse than proceeding most of the way through a carving to discover that the layers were wrong in the first place. Making a PLASTICINE model is one way to help determine the correct layers, or if this is inappropriate, careful marking is a good option.

LEATHER

For the carver, a supply of hide leather is very useful, although only small quantities are required at any one time.

Use firm hide leather for a STROP and soft KIDSKIN for a TOOL ROLL. Leather pouches can be made for individual tools to enable them to be carried safely. For example, when traveling to lumberyards to search for or test timber, or to an orchard or farm to examine a fallen tree, a 1-inch (25 mm) GOUGE is a handy tool to take. A leather sheath makes it safe to carry.

LEVERING

See L–05.
Using the carving tool as a lever is a common and very poor practice for a woodcarver. "Twisting" the tool is another similarly poor practice. Levering and twisting are techniques used to remove wood waste and sometimes the chisel itself from the wood, if it becomes stuck. Two things are likely to occur:
✔ The sharp edge of the tool is likely to break away, or if the tool is sufficiently buried in the wood it might break the shaft.
✔ If the wood at the place where the tool is twisted is weak, it will break and damage the carving.

L–05
Always remove the tool sideways and it will fall out if it is stuck, and never remove waste other than with an effective clean cut. If the cut is not good enough for the waste to come away freely, re-cut until it is. A levering action like this above will break the tool.

LIGHTING

Apart from the overhead or VERTICAL light in your carving environment, it is important there be a supply of CROSS LIGHT as well. Cross lighting creates shadows that enable us to see exactly the shapes we are creating. Cross lights should be moveable to give flexibility that creates shadows from all directions. Lights will get hot, so there is a danger of burning if care is not taken to maintain a safe distance from the work surface. Different light types have a different COLOR TEMPERATURE.

Natural sunlight is the very best for carving, particularly when the sun is low in the sky and therefore creates good shadow activity. Unfortunately these ideal conditions are short-lived each day!

To test your lighting system for effectiveness in creating high visibility, take some of your work out into the afternoon sun and see how much more you can "see'" in the natural cross light. Inadequate lighting of any kind will affect your ability to see, may cause headache, and in prolonged cases may damage your eyesight.

LINEN FOLD

See L–06.
The decoration known as the linen fold panel originated in Europe. It is a "classic" carving pattern, in the realm of Gothic tracery and acanthus leaves. The linen fold pattern may be made entirely with carving tools; however, it was commonly created by a combination of hand molding planes and gouges. The MOLDING PLANES were used to make the long troughs and ridges and the gouges to carve out the undercuts to create the folds at the top and the bottom.

In ecclesiastic carving the linen fold pattern was commonly used to decorate altars, pulpits, and door panels.

L–06
The linen fold pattern is an excellent and traditional decoration for panels of all kind.

LINSEED OIL

See L–07.

Linseed oil is extracted from the flax plant, the fibers from which are used to make linen. Linseed oil is an amber, colored liquid that darkens as it ages, and it has many uses in wood finishing. Used in boiled form it is a penetrating finish for anything from cricket bats to carved sculptures. It is used raw as a lubricant in the French polishing process, or as an additive for VARNISH. Raw linseed oil is thick and tends to be sticky and takes some time to dry. In boiled form it is thinner, penetrates faster, dries more quickly, and is therefore easier to apply and build up to the required sheen.

LONDON PATTERN

See L–08.

For the woodcarver the "London pattern" refers to a shape style for the chisel handle. This is a traditional handle fitting comfortably in the hand. There are variations on the London pattern from different manufacturers, and most incorporate a round portion. Some carvers criticize the "London pattern" handle for its ability to roll off

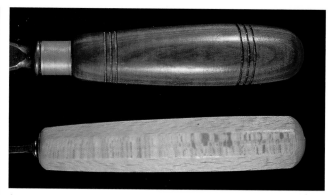

L–08
The London pattern is the handle at the top of the illustration. It is generally more comfortable than the hexagonal handle.

the workbench, and as a result prefer a hexagonal handle. This is the handle most commonly manufactured in today's environment, because it is easier and cheaper to make, although it is not necessarily the best or most comfortable shape.

LONG BENT

See L–09.

The long bent gouge, similar to the SHORT BENT gouge, is useful for access to awkward places. It is very useful for GROUNDWORK, and the inclusion of a reasonably flat gouge for this purpose will not be wasted in the tool kit for the relief carver. A LONG BEVEL is the best for most situations for which the long bent tool will be used. If it is

L–07
The piece of wood on the left of the illustration has been treated with one coat of linseed oil; the other piece of wood is bare. Oil finishes are excellent for woodcarvings.

76

L–09
Be careful when sharpening the long bent tool not to round off the cutting edge and, in effect, create a "short bent" high approach to the wood.

too short, it will raise the angle of approach of the tool too high into the wood and make it harder to use.

LONG BEVEL
See L–10.
The grinding of a long bevel on the carving chisel makes it thinner at the cutting end; therefore it is possible to make a finer and more razor-like edge. It also makes it weaker and more likely to chip or break. For this reason, long thin bevels are generally unsuitable for harder woods. The grinding of a CONCAVE BEVEL or a CONVEX BEVEL is a skill that the woodcarver must master. The alteration of bevels to suit certain circumstances such as hard or soft wood or design style is something that the carver must come to

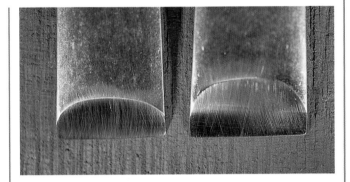

L–10
The same tool with a long or a short bevel will behave in quite different ways. It may be necessary to alter the bevel length to cope with different circumstances, such as hard timber (the left-hand bevel) or soft timber (the right-hand bevel).

M–01
It is important to ensure the bevel on the macaroni tool is the same length (or angle) on all three sides of the cutting edge.

terms with if he/she is to develop the skills for high-competency carving.

LOW RELIEF
Low relief is one of the different forms of RELIEF CARVING. It is to be distinguished from high relief and medium relief carving.

MACARONI
See M–01.
For the woodcarver, the macaroni chisel is a specialist shape used for cleaning out the sides of recesses. It may be used around the perimeter of panels. This sort of tool is not used frequently by the average carver, and is similar to the FLUTERONI. The sharpening of the macaroni is similar to the "V" TOOL or PARTING TOOL, and the bevel is on the outside.

MALLET

See M–02.

The mallet is one of the most important tools in the woodcarver's TOOL KIT. The carver will most likely need more than one mallet, depending on the type of work to be done. Carving mallets are round, tapered, and mostly made from wood. The carver's mallet is round so that irrespective of the position of it in relation to the end of the chisel handle, it will always present the same "face" to the handle. If it were flat like a carpenter's mallet, a glancing blow might result if the angle of strike were not straight end-on to the handle. This may cause accidental breakage or inaccurate cutting

M–02
Choose a mallet carefully to help avoid muscle injury. A special-shaped mallet may be necessary if arthritis is present in the arm or hand.

of the carving. Mallets of different weights are available for general use, very fine work, or large

M–03
Choose a marking method that does not make the pattern too hard to see. "Lead" (graphite) pencil is not always the best (second from the left).

sculpture. A mallet that is too light will cause muscle strain, as will one that is too heavy. A mallet that is top-heavy is more appropriate for large sculpture than one that has a center of balance closer to the hand for general use.

MARKING OUT

See M–03.

Transferring or marking out the design onto the wood will require different techniques depending on the circumstance:

✔ For dark woods, use a white pencil. "China-

graph" or crayon pencil is excellent for wood. It will not penetrate, and will not rub off accidentally.

✔ Carbonized paper is excellent for tracing patterns.

✔ Use painter's masking tape (it does not have permanent adhesive) to stabilize the drawing on the wood while it is being copied.

✔ Chalk is useful for larger sculptures, but be aware that its dust may penetrate the wood cells.

✔ Use different colors to mark out and distinguish

M–04
This maquette is about 8 inches (203mm) high, and was used to help design a garden sculpture four feet (1219mm) high.

MAQUETTE
See M–04.

A maquette is a model of a proposed larger carving. The maquette is used to establish the "look" of the final work, and is sometimes sold by the carver for additional revenue. Often it is made from clay, wax, or plaster as building up in these materials is faster than carving down in wood. If the maquette is to be re-used several times, it is best to make it from a material that will not disintegrate with handling. Wood is best, although some specialist MODELING waxes are excellent for this purpose. Unless great care is taken, plaster and clay are inappropriate for continuous use.

MIRROR IMAGES
See M–05.

Creating the mirror image is one of the great challenges for the woodcarver. To make the same image on one side of an architectural piece as the other is not easy, and indeed using a mirror may be a great help. SYMMETRY and uniformity are important in architectural carving, and using a mirror is a good way to help achieve them. Small differences in the same panel at either ends of a room will not be noticed, whereas side by side they may well be. This is not to excuse poor copying, but it does relieve the situation if necessary.

between different layers.
✔ Graphite pencil may be difficult to see in some lighting conditions and on some wood colors. Black fine-tipped felt pen or pencil is a good substitute.

MARQUETRY

Marquetry is inlaid work that may be done with different-colored woods, shell, and other materials. PARQUETRY and INTARSIA are not too dissimilar. For the carver, marquetry may be used as additional decoration for box lids and for frames and borders. It requires accurate cutting of both the cavity for the insert and of the insert itself. For restoration work, it is always advisable to seek replacement pieces for individual components of the pattern before commencing the restoration—especially if it requires removal of some pieces for re-gluing.

M–05
The farther away from one another two carvings are, the less the chances any dissimilarities will be noticed.

MISERICORD

See M–06.

A misericord is a small hinged seat in the choir stalls of churches. The underside of the seat, which shows when the seat is folded upright and not in use, was often carved with life scenes and humor from the period. The carvers were given plenty of latitude with their humor, as the carvings often mock the clergy as well as other aspects of daily life.

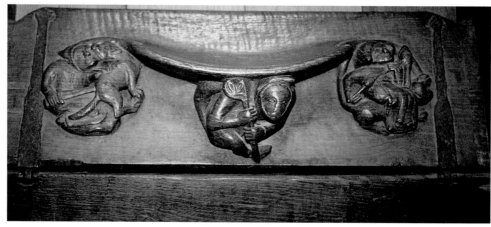

M–06

In a folded-up position, the misericord seat was also used as a rest during long church services.

MODELING

A model, sometimes also known as a MAQUETTE, is very useful preparation for the "real thing." Common modeling materials are modeling WAX, plaster of Paris, modeling clay, and PLASTICINE. There are a number of brand names available, particularly found in children's toy or art supply retailers. Models are generally faster to make than carvings, as they are built up from malleable and pliable materials, whereas carving is the process of "building down" from a non-replaceable material. If there is doubt as to the final shape of the carving, experiment with a model.

MOLDING

See M–07.

A molding is an ornamental contour applied along the length of a cornice, architrave, jamb or the like. Moldings of this nature are not generally made with carving chisels, as it is not possible to create long lengths evenly. The carver's CHISEL is, however, very useful for undertaking smaller repair work. Machinery using specially made cutting knives for milling the profile is the modern method, although hand MOLDING PLANES are still used for very small individual runs, particularly runs of picture frames.

MOLDING PLANES

See M–08.

Used for the creation of MOLDINGS, the hand molding plane is also used by the carver for making LINEN FOLDS. Individually shaped molding planes are generally no longer manufactured, and can only be procured through antique tool sellers. Some basic shapes such as the bead and the hollow illustrated make very useful additions to the carver's tool kit, especially for frame and border decoration.

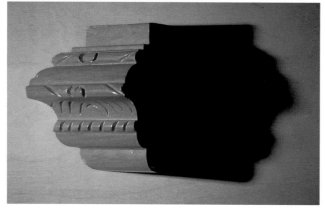

M–07

The addition of some hand carving to a purchased machine-made molding creates a unique decoration.

MOISTURE

Water occurs naturally in wood, and unseasoned wood may contain 30% or more of it. Wood has the ability to release moisture and take it up again, depending on the surrounding environment. As wood loses moisture it will generally shrink, and the reverse as it absorbs water. Because it can continually expand and contract, wood is best "stabilized" by sealing its surface. WET WOOD is generally softer than dry wood, and so it may be easier to carve, especially for denser species. When you create your carving, you will be increasing, sometimes considerably, the surface area of the wood exposed to the atmosphere (particularly with relief carving), so the wood will tend to release or take up moisture faster than it otherwise might. A plaque may WARP, for example, or the carved surface may CHECK. During carving, surface misting with an atomizer may reduce these tendencies and help control the seasoning process.

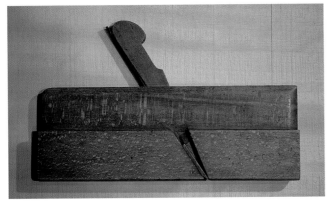

M–08
Special care must be taken to sharpen the blades on these tools so that their shape is the same contour as the wooden soul of the plane. If the two differ, the tool will not cut effectively, if at all.

N–01
A narrow-beam light may help highlight specific parts of a carving in progress. Personal preferences for lighting will vary from one carver to another.

NARROW BEAM

See N–01.
For the woodcarver, the establishment of the most appropriate style of LIGHTING is critical. There will be variation between one person and another, depending not only on personal preference but also on what is available for the carver to purchase. The person who does a lot of serious carving may well want different kinds of lighting for different circumstances, and part of this may be the choice between a wide-angle beam and a narrow-angle beam of light to carve by. The wider angle is the more useful as general light, while the narrow beam may be more appropriate for highlighting specific small areas where fine detail needs a concentrated effort.

NATURAL LIGHTING

Sunlight is by far the best to carve by, though as it is constantly varying with the earth's movement, it is not the most convenient LIGHTING. However, it is a good light source by which to judge your carving efforts. If your carving can stand the scrutiny of sunlight, it can more than survive the less effective nature of artificial light. Morning or afternoon sun will cast the longest shadows, the strongest being in the middle of the day with the sun overhead. You will see the effectiveness of natural light for carving, particularly if you compare it to FLUORESCENT lighting, which is a diffused, basically shadow-less light.

NEATSFOOT OIL

Neatsfoot oil is a pale yellow, almost odorless oil obtained by the boiling of cattle leg and hoof bones. It is a traditional leather softener and preservative. Woodworkers use neatsfoot oil as a lubricant for slip stones in the SHARPENING process. Historically, it was most likely one of the few suitable oils readily available. However, it does have some advantages over mineral oil. It is less irritating on skin, does not clog the pores of the stone quite as badly as mineral oil can, and it tends to float the ground metal particles away from the tool edge.

NICKING

See N–02.
Nicking is also known as notching. It is a common feature of 17th century oak furniture. To execute this pattern there are some particular techniques that need to be observed:
✔ The tool must be very sharp so as not to crush the end grain as it moves through to create the sides of the nick.
✔ The two side cuts must meet in the middle for even-sided and neat work.

N–03
Nulling is the fluted pattern around the outward-facing edge of the chair leg.

✔ The size and placement of the nick must be carefully measured and marked if necessary. Accurate indexing is required for round edges and a compass should be used.

NOTCHING

Notching is the same as NICKING.

NULLING

See N–03.
A series of small projections or recessions from the surface of the carving is called nulling. These are usually seen as a run of beads, flutes, or bosses. The creation of these decorations requires not only the accuracy of repetition,

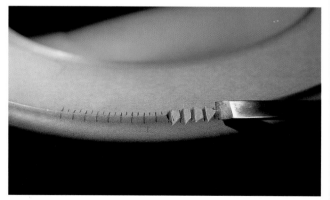

N–02
Accuracy and patience are required for neat notching.

but also the accuracy of uniform spacing or indexing. These sorts of repetitive carving need to be practiced over and over again to ensure uniformity. With this practice, the carver will develop his or her own special way of doing repetitive work. The choice of tool will most likely be somewhat different from one person to another, although the end results may be very similar.

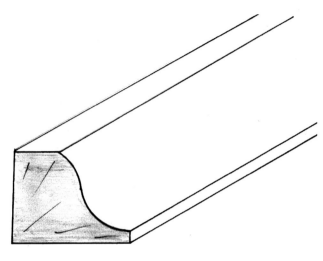

O–01
It is generally not a proposition to consider hand-making moldings in anything other than very short lengths. This is the traditional ogee pattern.

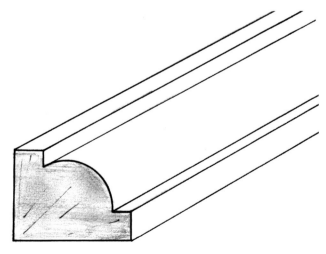

O–02
A repetitive pattern could be carved on the surface of the molding to decorate the plain surface. This is the traditional ovolo pattern.

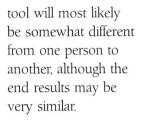

OGEE
See O–01 and O–02. The ogee and the ovolo moldings are classic shapes. If made by hand a MOLDING PLANE will be used for cutting the different curves. The hand-making of an ogee molding requires the use of a TEMPLATE for constant testing of the pattern. Hand carving such a molding would normally only be undertaken for small repair work or very short runs, because uniformity in long lengths is virtually impossible to achieve using carving gouges.

OIL GILDING
Oil gilding is a style of gilding that differs from the WATER GILDING principally in that the procedure for applying the gold leaf uses a sizing rather than distilled water. Oil gilding is also characteristically "duller" than water gilding. If there is any doubt as to the stability of the carved surface in normal atmospheric conditions, oil gilding may be the preferred option, as the sizing seals the surface from moisture.

OILSTONE
An oilstone is used for the SHARPENING phase of preparing the chisel for use. There are many different kinds of natural and synthetic oilstone available for the carver, and the best is a small SLIP STONE, rather than the more common BENCH STONE. "Oil," often machine oil, is used as the lubricant, which acts to help keep the area of the stone being used for the grinding clear of metal filings from the tool. NEATSFOOT OIL is a popular choice for

O–03
This heavily carved oriel window is typical of medieval times.

cess oil is left sitting on the surface, dust may be attracted to the timber. Dust is difficult to remove from wood pores. A soft sheen will result from continued light applications of orange oil.

ORIEL WINDOW
See O–03.
An oriel window is a large window built out from a wall and resting on a bracket or CORBEL. It resembles a bay window. These windows were common in ancient architecture and were often elaborately carved.

OVERLAY
See O–04.
The overlay and the TEMPLATE are commonly used for artwork and marking out when individual features need to be separately described or drawn. Completed on transparent tracing paper, the individual components are laid over one another so that the whole picture can be seen. When preparing overlays, always mark on each overlay a positioning guide in at least two

tool sharpening. Some slip stones use water as the lubricant and are called WATERSTONES.

OLIVE OIL
A wide variety of oil finishes are available to the carver. Of them, fruit and nut oils are popular, and these include olive oil, ORANGE OIL, and TUNG oil. One of the most appropriate applications for olive oil is as a finish for wooden utensils that are to be

used in the kitchen—salad servers, platters, breadboards and so on. The oil will penetrate and offer some protection to the timber; however, frequent applications will be needed as the oil will be washed off with modern kitchen detergents. Too much oil applied at one time may cause a rancid odor if it is left to degenerate. Apply a light covering, wiping off the excess.

ORANGE OIL
Orange oil is a yellow liquid with the distinctive odor of the orange. Unlike OLIVE OIL, orange oil will impart a golden hue to light-colored timbers, and will give a natural-looking richness to darker woods. When using oils, particularly thick oils like TUNG oil, do not apply too much at one time. Some grain raising may occur with some woods, and if ex-

places if not each corner, so that each drawing can be aligned in the same place over the other drawing every time they are used. A simple crosshair is easiest.

OXALIC ACID

Oxalic acid is a mild bleaching agent and is usually used in a 10% solution with hot distilled water or methylated spirits (denatured ALCOHOL). It may give a pink tinge to some species, and to be effective it may require several applications, each being washed off after about 15 minutes. It is poisonous and gloves should be worn and the sanding dust should not be inhaled. It may be used to generally lighten the color of the wood, or to remove stains. If bleaches of any kind are to be used, it is important to test them on a scrap of the same species before applying to your carving.

OXIDIZE

See O–05.
The chemical reaction of the combination of a substance with oxygen is the most prolific natural

O–05
It is important to realize that the wood surface of a carving will oxidize and change color. The freshly cut kauri pine (*Agathis microstachya*) on the top of this illustration will eventually oxidize to the color of the rough-sawn piece from which it was cut.

chemical activity. Wood-carving tool steel will oxidize and form RUST, to be avoided at all costs. Wood itself undergoes a transformation of color as the result of the oxidation of polyphenolic compounds into quinones. Freshly cut sapwood may take on a brown color due to oxidation processes similar to when an apple is cut. As wood ages, its exposure to the atmosphere will result in this oxidation process taking place, and it may become lighter and eventually go gray like the shingles and shakes on buildings, or darker as in the case of Radiata pine (*Pinus radiata*).

O–04
It is imperative that each overlay is placed accurately over the previous drawing.

P–01
The palm chisel is sharpened in the same way as any other chisel.

PALM CHISELS

See P–01 and P–02.
Palm chisels are small tools that have a flat on one side of a bulbous handle. This flat area allows the handle to be lowered quite close to the surface of the wood being cut, to enable very fine, shallow carving to take place. These tools are commonly used for engraving a WOODCUT for printing. The tool is held in the palm of the hand and is moved by pushing it with the thumb and sliding it against the index finger. Special control skill needs to be developed because the tool is used one-handed. This is best practiced on softer woods first; then "graduate" to close end-grain cut woods like fruit woods.

PANTOGRAPH

See P–03.
A pantograph is used for enlarging or reducing patterns. Tracing around an outline with the stylus on one axis, the movement is translated through the moving arms to the pencil, which redraws either larger or smaller, depending on the relative position of the arms. Great skill is needed to operate a pantograph, and this has been replaced by the technology of the photocopier and computer for high-speed reproduction.

P–02
Use the palm chisel in a one-handed operation—for best control, push the blade of the tool along the inside of the thumb.

PARING

Of all tool techniques, the most common for woodcarving is "digging" into the wood with a mallet and chisel. The carver must also develop considerable skill at trimming surfaces and edges with fine strokes from very finely honed finishing tools. This is the skill of paring. Mostly done with a SKEW or a KNIFE, patiently paring off fine, accurate shavings creates a smooth but lightly textured surface and enables the carver to carefully manipulate the wood to the desired shape. Good tool control with the fingers and a stress-free, relaxed POSTURE are great advantages when paring.

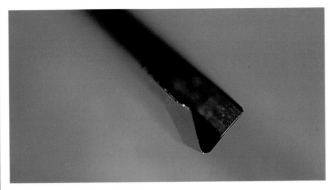

P–04

If the inside and outside of the parting tool are not ground to the same shape, a blunt spot will be created at the point or apex of the "V" and it will tear instead of cutting cleanly.

PARQUETRY

Parquetry is the making of patterns, primarily geometric, by assembling different colors of wood together. Mostly a technique used for decorative floors, the individual pieces form the full thickness of the floor covering. This technique is not to be confused with INTARSIA or MARQUETRY, both of which are decorative techniques of inlaying pieces into a carrier surface.

PARTING TOOL

See P–04.

The parting tool is the traditional name for the "V" TOOL. Parting tools are available as straight, long bent, and short bent. They require special attention to their sharpening–generally the inside of the "V" is not a pointed curve, but a fine "U" shape. It is important to ensure the outside of the "V" is sharpened to the same shape as the inside, and this is achieved by rolling the tool over the wheel or stone in the same manner as a GOUGE.

PATERA

See P–05.

A patera was a sacrificial plate or dish used by ancient Romans for liquid offerings. In woodcarving it is an ornamental relief design that was commonly used in border patterns,

P–03

Most modern woodcarvers would never have seen a pantograph. Great skill is needed for accurate enlargement or reduction.

P–05

This carving is from a decorative panel approximately 1000 years old.

decorative wall panels, and friezes for many centuries. Sometimes it is possible to track the origins of carvings by identifying particular features and matching them to other historically known facts.

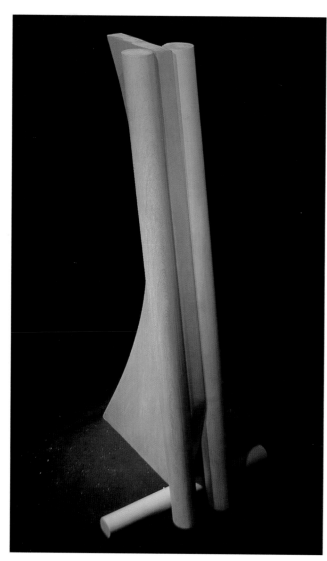

P–06
The design of a pedestal must be in harmony with the sculpture it intends to support. It is inevitably a part of the finished display.

PATINA

A patina is a mellowed surface finish usually the result of age and use. It is particularly a feature of old furniture. It is possible to recreate such a finish by the frequent application of thin wax, rubbed in with the fingers. Over a short time it may be possible to give the appearance of "used old age." The color of the wood is also important, as older wood tends to be darker than fresher wood. Coloration with SHELLAC may enhance the ability to quickly achieve a mellowed look.

PEDESTAL

See P–06.
For large sculptures that need to be displayed on a stand, a pedestal is the common way. The design of the pedestal is critical to the appeal of the sculpture, and for its safety. For this reason, it is necessary to consider at least the following:

✔ The pedestal must be at the right height for the best viewing of the work.
✔ The pedestal design must not "steal the show" from the sculpture.
✔ The pedestal design must be suitable for the nature of the carving and not in design conflict with it.
✔ The pedestal must be stable.

PEG

"Polyethylene glycol" is one of several chemical seasoning agents. These agents require soaking the wood in a hygroscopic chemical (one that attracts moisture). Other agents are common salt (sodium chloride) and urea. PEG and urea also have a bulking effect by replacing some of the water that is removed, helping to reduce CELL shrinkage. Salt will introduce a corrosive element. Whether you use these or other chemical methods, it is important to follow all safety instructions that may accompany the manufactured product. In addition, be sure to find out the effect of the chemical on the color, texture, and residual strength of the wood. It may be that the species you wish to carve becomes too brittle due to cell collapse.

PEROXIDE

Hydrogen peroxide, a well-known bleach for hair, is present in many households. In conjunction with household ammonia, it can be an effective timber bleach. Apply concentrated ammonia to the wood, let it soak in for an hour or so, and make sure the surface is dry. Add a 30% solution of hydrogen peroxide, and let it dry. Repeat applications may be needed of both chemicals. Do not mix the two together, and wear protective clothing. Test your bleaching process on a scrap of timber first rather than spoil the carving with poor bleaching technique. OXALIC ACID may be more effective as a bleach on many species.

PIERCED RELIEF
See P–07.
Piercing or cutting through to make pierced relief is commonly used in furniture design. The piercing is done with a SCROLL SAW or COPING SAW. For pierced designs consideration must be given to the thickness of the wood and the location of the cut-out areas. Piercing clearly weakens the wood, so the remaining areas must be arranged so that they maximize the residual strength. Large open areas should be avoided, so should very thin cross sections, and there should be as many "junctions" as possible.

PIGMENTS
Pigments may be natural or synthetic, and are generally used to color

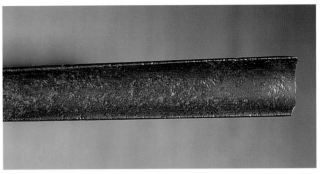

P–08
Storing tools in a damp environment, for example on or near the garage floor, is a potential cause of rust—as is the sweat from hands.

surface finishes such as paint. They may be used to color wood, and should be tested first to ensure their application produces the desired effect. There are many colors and varieties available from art supply retailers. It is important to follow manufacturer's instructions, as some pigments are poisonous. If applied directly to timber, the pigment will often penetrate into the cell cavity and fill it with color, leaving the surface unaffected. Uneven coloring is the result. It may be necessary to seal the carved surface first, before adding color. It is very important to test on an offcut, as the addition of pigment directly to wood will most likely be permanent.

PITTED TOOLS
See P–08.
RUST damage can ruin a carving chisel very quickly. A blade that has been pitted by rust cannot be sharpened to a fine edge, as a corroded surface area means there is no continuity of steel. Rust is the OXIDATION of the iron in the steel, and it is caused by the presence of water. Water from the atmosphere is often sufficient to start the rusting process, so consistent wet weather is a sign to check your tools. After using tools, wipe them with a dry cloth and store in a dry place such as a TOOL ROLL or tool drawer. RUST PREVENTION is possible by coating the tool steel with a water repellent.

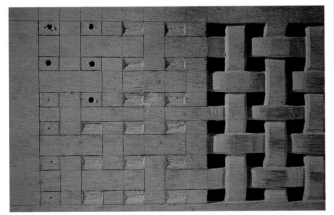

P–07
Pierced relief can produce attractive results; however, the piercing stage can also be very repetitive and tedious, as with this cane-weave pattern for a chair splat.

PLASTICINE

See P–09.

Plasticine is a very good MODELING medium. Some brands of plasticine are better than others, inasmuch as they have a higher melting point, and will not sag under the temperature of a warm summer day. A low melting point may also be an advantage of plasticine, as it will easily soften in the warmth of the hands. Plasticine, like WAX and clay, is normally molded by hand, or cut and shaped with knives or spatulas. Make some wooden knives out of thin strips of wood, and shape them to your own specifications.

P–09
Plasticine is sometimes too soft to hold its shape and make an effective model of a proposed carving.

PLUG

See P–10.

A wooden plug is perfect for repairing knotholes and other damage in your carving. Consideration will need to be given to the direction of the GRAIN, and to whether there will be any visual disadvantage in the direction of the grain of the plug being different from that of the body of the wood. The plug is made as a tapered piece that is tapped in as far as it will go without further damaging the wood. The direction of the grain in the plug will be the opposite of the direction in the block. If this is unacceptable, it is necessary to cut the plug from end-grain wood. An end-grain plug is very weak, and when it is being tapped into place great care must be taken not to break or fracture it.

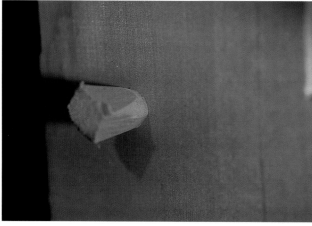

P–10
Fill grub and knotholes with either an end-grain or long-grain plug, then carve it off.

PLYWOOD

Plywood is made by LAMINATING a number of VENEERS with the grain direction alternated with each added layer. Plywood is not a recommended carving medium. First, the continually changing grain direction makes it exceptionally difficult to carve to any depth. Second, the glue that is used is often damaging to tools.

POLISH

Most wood polishes are in the form of creamy synthetic or natural waxes of varying densities. Ingredient lists vary considerably, some allowing for high shine with ingredients such as CARNAUBA, others for none. Some require the wood surface to be sealed first for best polishing results, others may have sealing ingredients in them. Thin wax will tend to soak straight into unsealed timber, and many, many applications may be required to obtain the desired result. Testing is the best method to ensure the finish you require for the carved object. Polishing waxes should be applied sparingly in a number of coats so as not to get a sudden buildup that will remain thick, sticky, unattractive and collect dust. Care should be taken not to get too much wax in corners and grooves. It may need to be cleaned out with a sharp instrument.

POLISHING CUT
See P–11.
With many species, a finely honed carving tool when passed through it will "polish" the surface. Natural wax and RESIN in the wood, a fine close grain, and a polished tool edge that doesn't tear or scrape but cuts clean through all combine to make a shiny cut surface. Develop a personalized "sharpness test" by finding a species that reacts this way. Try Indonesian jelutong, Australian rose mahogany, American black walnut, European lime, or English oak.

POSTURE
See P–12.
The way we sit or stand is of great importance while carving. A bench that is too low for the carver's height will cause

P–12
This carver is resting on his left forearm, not only increasing tool control but also helping prevent backache.

P–11
The shiny cut made in this piece of New Guinea kwila (*Intsia bijuga*) indicates a finely sharpened tool cutting in harmony with the grain characteristics of the wood.

back problems, and slouching may do the same. Resting hands and forearms on the carving or the BENCH will give greater tool control and reduce arm muscle fatigue. Holding a tool down low may do the same. It is important to try different bench heights and stool or chair heights if you prefer sitting. If standing for long periods, make sure the floor has some "give" in it or a covering like very thick rubber matting that will have sufficient movement to reduce or remove leg fatigue.

POUND

Wood, sold in log or block form, is often sold by the KILO, and not by linear measurement.

PROFILE

See P–13.
Especially for CARVING IN THE ROUND, it is very important to gain an early understanding of the visualization of the profile of the subject. As you rotate the view around an irregular-shaped object, the profile will change accordingly. If the subject is a geo-metric shape such as a sphere, the profile will remain the same throughout the rotation on any plane. To appre-ciate how these changing views connect together to form the whole, it is necessary to accept that irrespective of the actual location of a body part on an animal (for exam-ple) any profile at any time in its rotation is the same from one side as from the other. In other words, opposing 180-degree views are identi-cal. So each "snapshot" that might be taken of a particular view creates a profile that is the same when viewed from the opposite side. Joining all the profiles together cre-ates the whole. Not only should the profiles be examined horizontally, but they should also be viewed from each differ-ent ELEVATION.

PROFILE GAUGE

See P–14.
For copying or transfer-ring profiles from origi-nal to new work, a profile gauge is invalu-able. The wire pins slide in the stock, and press-ing the gauge onto the surface of the original will transfer the profile to these wires; a tracing can be made onto thin wood for a permanent TEM-PLATE. The wires can easily bend or come right out, so care needs to be taken using this tool, and storage in a safe place is essential.

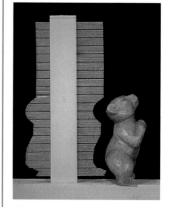

P–14
A profile gauge adds consider-able ease to the copying of shapes.

PUMICE

See P–15.
Pumice is a spongy gray-colored light porous vol-canic rock that can easily be ground into very fine grain sizes. It is used as an abrasive and a FILLER. For example, it might be used on a STROP for polishing tool surfaces, or as a substi-tute for abrasive paper on timber or SHELLAC. It is effective in very fine particle size used with leather and water as a smoothing agent be-tween coats of varnish

P–13
The profile front to back is the same as that from back to front, provided the two views are at 180 degrees to one another.

or other surface finishes. For your carved surface—before application of a finish such as shellac—pumice may be an effective grain filler. It will tend to take on the color of the shellac and fill the cells of the wood, making a good base for a fine finish.

PUNCH

See P–16.
In woodwork there are different styles of punches for different applications, such as center marking and counter punching. In woodcarving, punches are used for creating decorative backgrounds. Punching is sometimes referred to as stamping. Punches may vary from simple "dots" to more fancy

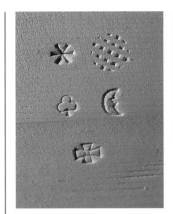

P–16
Often, a simple "dot" punch was used to disguise a damaged or poorly carved background. Many other patterns are also available for decorative work.

outlines. It is important to take care that the punching is not done so heavily that it damages the surface by breaking the fibers and generally "chewing" it.

PUTTY

Putty is manufactured from a wide variety of materials, and is a common product for filling gaps and holes in wood surfaces, particularly before painting. Wood-colored putty may be used to repair surfaces that are to have a "natural look" finish. In such cases, it is recommended that the putty be tested on a mock repair to ensure not only an acceptable color match, but to check that the putty does not shrink below the surface as its solvent dries. A check should also be made to ensure the putty will sustain any other finish that might be needed for the work, such as shellac or wax.

PYROGRAPHY

See P–17.
Pyrography is the burning of a design into the surface of wood. It is done with a hot tip from a pyrograph, with the heat produced and controlled electrically. Different sizes and shapes of burning tips can be attached to the heating element, which works in a way similar to an electric soldering iron. Pyrography is often added to woodcarvings as a decorative feature, such as feathering on decoy ducks. Pyrography is most visible on lighter-colored woods, and some woods will react better than others to this technique. For this reason, testing should be undertaken before being applied to the finished piece.

P–15
The original pumice (top left) may be ground into a coarse powder (bottom left) or a superfine powder (bottom right) for polishing.

P–17
This pyrograph is electrically heated. The line pattern work in Illustration I–12 was done with a hot poker heated over coals from a fire.

Answers to the twenty most asked questions about woodcarving

1
Which wood should I use?

Some woods are more suitable for certain things than others. A logical process of elimination will be the best way to determine which wood is the best for a particular project, combined with a good knowledge of what woods are available. A wood that is very dense and heavy will be unsuitable for a large carved picture frame to be hung on a wall. A wood that is crumbly and brittle will not sustain very fine detailed carving, and one that is pulpy will not be suitable for a rocking horse. If it is for furniture, it will need to be resilient and stand a little rough treatment.

If color is important, this will dictate to a large extent the choices that are available. Begin to answer your Which Wood? question with an open mind. Start by making a wood "specification" list, including all the things you can think of that are relevant, and search out all the available alternatives. Many specialist suppliers have sample sets that may help, and some mail-order catalogues carry good descriptions of what a particular wood can be used for. The local library may have books that will assist. One way to find the right answer is to experiment with as many samples as possible.

2
What subject can I carve?

This will largely depend on what wood is available and the skills of the individual carver. The novice carver should adopt an outlook for design choice that will enable a learning curve to be embarked upon that will not result in frustration on the one hand or boredom on the other. A simple leaf or flower is a good starting point for RE-LIEF CARVING, and a simple shape such as a decoy duck is a good starting point for CARVING IN THE ROUND. Progress from a leaf by adding a flower, for example, and from a floating duck by creating a standing goose. Avoid a lot of detail to start with, creating basic shapes only.

By choosing in this manner, progress is sustainable and enjoyable. Unless skills of observation and technique are fairly well advanced, for relief carving avoid subjects that include perspective and depth illusion or are just simply complicated; and for carving in the round avoid faces, hands, feet, and realism generally.

Successful relief carving will require tool skills and shadow development that need to be acquired over time by experimentation. Successful carving in the round will require experimentation to develop observation and visualization skills.

3
What tools do I need?

Individual carvers will develop their own specific TOOL KIT needs. No two carvers will be identical. For this reason, avoid purchasing a manufacturer's predetermined set of tools. Buy individual tools as and when they are needed, and considerable waste may be avoided. In general, more tools will be needed for relief carving than in the round, although once again individual style and the actual design will dictate this.

As a starting point, however, a standard straight-shafted 6mm, 10mm, and 20mm slightly curved GOUGE, an 8mm PARTING TOOL, and a 3mm and 6mm FLUTER will be enough to start the novice in both

Q–01
A comfortable posture such as this is essential for good tool control. Without it, carving is an awkward activity.

Q–02
Holding the tool at the top of the handle like this will cause it to wobble around and no control will be achieved.

Q–03
This is a better place to hold the tool, but do not grasp it so tightly as to "strangle" it.

Q–04
Holding the tool down low and resting the forearm on the carving offers great control.

RELIEF CARVING and CARVING IN THE ROUND. These are all basic tools and will not be wasted. Add a MALLET, a SLIP STONE and STROP, and a beginner's kit is in place. A considerable amount of work can be done with these tools, before any further purchases will be necessary.

4
Is this how you hold a chisel?

See Q–01 to Q–10.
There are no rules about holding carving tools. However, there are some principles that when followed will make things a lot easier:

Here is a checklist of tips on proper chisel use:
✔ The carver must be comfortable, without stress on the back.
✔ Do not grip the tool like a vise. A relaxed approach will ensure better tool control.
✔ Resting the hands on the wood will make for a more comfortable posture and also give better tool control.
✔ Do not tense or straighten the fingers. Keep them rounded.
✔ Hold the tool down low near the cutting edge, not right up on the handle. This will give greater control and be more comfortable. A tool held high will tend to wobble around too much.

Q–05
In this "right-handed" illustration, the left hand is steering the skew in a paring action, while the right hand controls it.

Q–08
A far more relaxed hand action will help ensure good results.

Q–06
This tool has a knob or knurl on the handle for the thumb. The thumb is the strongest "finger" in the hand, and if used like this helps produce very accurate results.

Q–09
Push the knife away from the body, and if possible rest the end of the wood on a bench.

Q–07
This knife is being held in a very tight and uncomfortable way. There is too much tension in the index finger.

Q–10
For great control and accuracy, push the blade of the knife with the thumb to prevent it slipping.

5
What Is a skew for?

The SKEW is the only carving tool that can be used effectively and easily to create any convex curve. It is used in a PARING or slicing action. Its double-sided bevel means it can be flipped over so the carver can reverse direction easily for right- or left-handed use. It can also be used as a KNIFE, or for getting into difficult corners to clean them out. It may take a little time; however, it is well worthwhile mastering this versatile tool.

6
Is this chisel blunt?

A blunt carving tool will become evident very quickly. It will make a TEARING CUT on the surface, or it may make a grating sound and SCRATCH the surface, and more energy will be required to push it through the wood than if it were sharp. Because it is tearing the wood, it will start to CHIP fine edges, and generally damage will accompany each cut. The development of a standard test for sharpness is recommended, and tool SHARPENING must be practiced and developed into a fine art by the carver. Choose a readily available soft timber such as jelutong (*Dyera costulata*), lime (*Tilia* spp.), or basswood (*Tilia* spp.), and a blunt tool as well as a sharp tool. The two different tools will make a different sound in the same wood, there will be a different visual end result, and there will be noticeably different energy requirements to get each one to cut. Let sight, sound, and feel be the judges!

7
How do I sharpen this "V" tool?

See Q–11.
The PARTING TOOL, or "V" tool, is often touted as the most difficult carving tool for SHARPENING; however, it really isn't that hard at all. Look at the sharp end of the tool end-on. If the tool is incorrectly sharp-

Q–11
Avoid grinding the apex of the parting tool in a way that will cut a hole in it. Great care is needed to clean a burr from the inside of these tools.

ened and it is tearing at the wood, the inside of the tool is not the same shape as the outside at the apex. Incorrectly sharpened, the inside will be a very small curve, and the outside will be ground to a pointed "V." Between the two is the blunt spot that is causing the trouble. The two edges must also be HONED.

To sharpen the tool correctly, treat it as nothing more than a very acute GOUGE. Sharpen the apex on the outside to the correct curve (one that matches the inside curve) by rolling the tool over the apex on the slip stone in the same way a gouge or FLUTER is rolled over the stone. If the inside of the tool needs some attention— which it will if a burr begins to appear (it can easily be felt with a finger)—be very careful using a fine-edged slip stone not to dig a hole through the apex. If this occurs, the tool will have to be ground flat and re-sharpened. Make sure the bevel on each side of the tool is not too short (about ¼ inch for a ½-inch tool is suitable for average work), otherwise the approach of the tool into the timber will be too steep and the tool may be difficult to use. Sometimes the tool will wear so that a pointed prow like that on a boat appears at the apex. It will be necessary to grind this off and re-shape the tool, otherwise it may break and the tool will start to tear at the wood.

8
How do I get started?

See the letter U for a comprehensive coverage of the order of proceeding.

9
What should I put on this carving when it is finished?

Wood finishes available to the modern wood-carver are many and varied. They may be natural coatings such as SHELLAC that is used for VARNISH, or WAX and RESIN from plants and trees. OILS are made from fruits and nuts of many species, and synthetic finishes vary from mat to high gloss, and they may penetrate or simply seal the surface. To help decide which one to use, it will be necessary to decide whether the finish is to be a protective coating from water, ALCOHOL, or other environmental influence, such as dust.

Manufacturer's instructions should give the information necessary to eliminate inappropriate finishes. As a generalization, natural finishes are not particularly resistant to water, alcohol, or heat.

10
Which tool do I use?

See the letter U.
The choice of tool for a particular activity will depend very much on the individual. As a general principle, the more experienced the carver, the fewer number of tools will be essential except perhaps for highly specialized activity. The experienced carver is able to achieve considerable versatility from a single tool. The more the experience, often the larger the tools that are used, because they are easier to handle and can cover a greater range of projects. It is important therefore not to rush in and purchase tools that may be outgrown quickly.

Each carver will also develop an individual style different from other carvers, and favorite tools will emerge. It is important that the carver experiment as much as possible with a range of tools. If this is not possible, obtain a catalog of shapes and give careful consideration to personal preferences, bearing in mind the two principles of (1) not too many and (2) bigger might be better in the longer term.

11
Can I carve this wood?

While it might sound trite, the reality is that any wood can be carved. Some are of course easier than others to carve, and the choice of tool and/or some modification of tool bevel shape may make difficult ones easier.

A very hard wood will be easier to carve with a heavier mallet that will give more power to each strike, and with a tool that is strongly built. For example, a straight-sided gouge is stronger than a FISHTAIL of the same sweep. The fishtail may well break or bend if used in a hard wood with a heavy mallet. If the wood chips or causes serration on the face of the tool, this can be almost if not completely stopped by altering the bevel shape. First, place a secondary BEVEL on the inside of the tool. This will make the thickness of the steel at the sharp end greater, therefore stronger. Placing a second bevel on the inside increases strength without altering the angle of approach of the tool to the wood, because the primary or original bevel has not been altered. It will be necessary to re-hone the tool after adding the second bevel. If the tool still gets damaged in the wood, then make the primary or original bevel shorter, and if this still doesn't succeed, make it slightly more convex. This will alter the angle of approach, but at the same time makes the tool edge stronger still.

For softer woods, the opposite bevel shape is most likely the best. There is no need for a secondary bevel, and a flatter or even a flat bevel may be best. The longer and thinner the bevel, the finer the sharp edge, and possibly the better the performance in softer wood. It is a matter of experimentation, all of the adjustments mentioned being only small ones. None of them need to be exaggerated.

It should also be noted that the tool steel has an impact on its ability to perform satisfactorily in harder wood. Hard and brittle steel is more likely to chip than slightly softer steel. Hardness varies by brand, so experimentation is necessary with this too. If the wood is WET, it will be easier to carve than when dry, so for some work, such as a SCULP-TURE in a very dense wood, it may be better to carve it from unseasoned stock.

12
Is this design too hard to carve?

This is a judgment that can only be made by consideration of issues such as: In which wood? With what skill level? and What are the design practicalities? Each of these issues is interdependent, and equilibrium between them will dictate the judgment. The improbability of design may be the easiest to cope with. Designs with multiple layers, clusters of fine tips, or great depth are unlikely candidates. Carving complex designs with these elements may require making individual components or dissecting the pattern into sections and assembling them.

Lower skill levels may be best suited to chunky carvings in the round such as simple animal shapes, or relief carvings of small groups of leaves, or simple flowers. Skills are developed with experimentation and practice, and each person has different aptitude and available time to acquire these. The available wood will have a major impact on the appropriateness of design. For example, coarse-grain hardwood is not appropriate for fine detail, which is better done in fine, close-grain softwood.

13
Where can I get designs?

In the absence of drawing skills with which one might create his own original patterns for carving, there is often an apparent void of carving patterns. Realistically, there are many sources of material. But before we move on to them, let's not dismiss the "inability to draw" attitude. The drawing skill required to create a carving pattern is not that of a professional artist. Yes, the line has to be the right shape and in the right place, but it is not necessary to be able to reproduce all the illu-sions of shadow and depth on paper. It is necessary to know where they are, but not to be able to draw them.

It is more than likely that every person is capable of copying shapes. Draw a leaf from the garden by tracing around it. Or a linen fold could be copied from a cloth hanging on a chair back, by drawing the ridges or highlights on paper. Certainly with some patience and an hour or two, the person who "can't draw anything" will no doubt be amazed at what is actually possible. Failing that, here are some key sources of material:

✔ For floral patterns of all kinds, try embroidery and tapestry pattern books. Line drawings are very common, and they are ideal for tracing on to wood. Choose patterns that aren't too fine and delicate to start with, and ones that don't have many, if any, "layers."

✔ For animals and birds, children's books are excellent. Look for the ones that are for painting or coloring in with pencil or crayon. Once again, these are often simple line drawings.

14
How can I hold this carving still?

This is a most important question from the safety point of view. It is essential that one hand does not hold the carving and the other the chisel. In some situations, such as CHIP CARVING, this is appropriate; however, an accidental cut across the hand with a chisel can cause permanent injury.

The simple precaution of a firm holding device makes the activity perfectly safe. There are many commercial specialist devices available. However, often the best are the simple ones that can be made in the workshop. Using a CAM or a BASE-BOARD is an ideal method for relief carving. For carving in the round, two screws from the bottom up, to hold the piece on a baseboard, is the easiest method. The piece will probably turn around if only one screw is used. CLAMP the board to a bench, or hold it in a VISE.

15
Should I start in relief or in the round?

RELIEF CARVING is all about the creation of SHADOW. Shadows give the illusion of shape and depth to an otherwise flat surface. The deeper the carving in relief, the more the carving approaches what is called "high relief." Relief carving is like painting a picture with shadow. It is technically demanding and as such will develop good tool handling and design interpretation skills.

CARVING IN THE ROUND is about the use of all dimensions to create freestanding form. It is demanding on visualization and as such will develop good observation skills. It generally uses fewer tools than relief; however, this will depend on the subject matter.

Neither one is more difficult than the other. They are both different, require different approaches, and develop different skills.

As relief is technically more complex, particu-larly with tool handling skills, it is considered the best to start with, although it is certainly not essential. The new carver should try both, to see what personal preferences emerge.

16
What sharpening stone should I use?

As with most tools, there are many sizes and shapes of SHARPENING stones, and they can be synthetic or natural. Some are for use on a tabletop and are generally referred to as "BENCH STONES," and others are for holding in the hand and are known as "SLIP STONES."

Bench stones are generally inappropriate for carving tools, mainly because it is not possible to see the BEVEL while grinding takes place. A bench stone is designed for sharpening flat blades at constant angles, like plane irons and carpenters chisels. For carving tools, it is essential to be able to see what you are doing, as the bevel is generally a concave curve laterally, and may have a slightly convex curve longitudinally. A small hand-held stone is ideal. It allows for plenty of vision, and is very light and easy to use.

17
Which brand of chisel is best?

There is no satisfactory answer to this question, except to say that if the tool performs in the manner desired, then it is the right brand. The composition of the STEEL in modern tools varies significantly between manufacturers, and, as a general guide, the cheaper tool has softer steel that will not stand up to the rigors of carving, especially in harder wood and with a mallet. The chisel may require constant sharpening, or be so soft that it will not hold an edge at all. Dearer tools will probably be more satisfactory, be better tempered, and be made from an ALLOY. They will generally be more substantial and more comfortable to hold. Very old tools of the antique variety are probably unsatisfactory, as the tool steel may have deteriorated and become weak or they may have worn beyond the tempered area, rendering them essentially useless.

18
Where can I find wood for carving?

In many countries of the world, wood is a scarce if not almost nonexistent asset. In others, there is an almost never-ending supply for the woodcarver. There is an enormous imbalance. Fortunately, though, there is one thing in the woodcarver's favor. Woodcarving is not an activity that can effectively be done in a hurry, so great amounts of wood aren't needed all at once, and in the majority of cases a carving requires only a small amount of wood.

In high residential areas, wood can often be obtained (apart from local specialist lumberyards) from local city councils, who have parks and gardens

departments. Trees are always being lopped or removed and the timber is often chipped for recycling. It would be a rare gardener who wouldn't give a block or two to a woodcarver!

"Tree doctors" are another good source of wood. They are always in contact with different species that may only end up in the mulcher.

If you know a farmer, then you may have a wonderful source of pieces of native species and many fruit and nut trees.

Check out the nearest timber mills—they may not commercially mill to sizes that you want, but they often burn or pulp what you do. All you need to know is where to turn up with a friendly smile and maybe get a begged or borrowed chain saw.

If it is thin planks of hardwood you need, check your nearest fencing contractor. Or a nearby furniture repairer or restorer. Amazing timbers can be rescued from old furniture destined for the dumpster.

For blocks, check your nearest firewood sup-

plier. And building demolition contractors are a great source of thick planks and beams.

There is never a shortage of wood for carving!

19
What does the other side look like?

This is one of the most asked questions when carving in the round from a photograph, where you have only one view to work from. There is no easy answer to the question. Familiarity with the subject matter is about the only way to achieve a satisfactory result, as this will allow logic to produce a significant amount of the answer.

It really is imperative to develop strong observation skills and become familiar with as much as possible about a subject to re-create a satisfactory version of it. There are no shortcuts and no quick fixes. Go to a zoo if necessary. Or go to an aviary. Observation and familiarization are the keys to successful re-creation.

20
How much Is my carving worth?

The question for which there is only one very uninformative answer—a carving is worth what someone will pay for it! Most likely the only certainty is that unless the work is produced by a carver who has achieved a reputation in the marketplace, and unless the carver is competent and fast, there will be no "satisfactory" compensation for the hours of effort sustained to achieve the desired end result. The price of art is a much vexed question, most artists bemoaning a fair return for labor and creativity.

It is of great importance that the carver who wishes to earn income from his/her work be very aware of the market in which the works are to be sold, not only in terms of supply but also of demand in the first place. To see what other people are "selling" their work for is not enough. Chances are they are not selling anything much at all. "On display" in a shop doesn't mean the works are "selling." It may be necessary to search out and sometimes create a new market. Certainly it is important that careful thought be given to ensure the carver's work is unique, and priced so that it is within the reach of those who would find it desirable.

Pricing for quotation on commission work is also a vexing question. Carvers with established clientele and pricing structures may not be the ones to follow. Lower pricing to gain a foothold and the opportunity to achieve a reputation may be a considered approach for a new entry into the marketplace, but care needs to be taken not to under-price so as to create an artificially low and cheap image that cannot be easily upgraded. Price undercutting is often a recipe for failure.

RAKED SHOULDER
See R–01.
There are many theories as to the "correct" tool design for woodcarving.

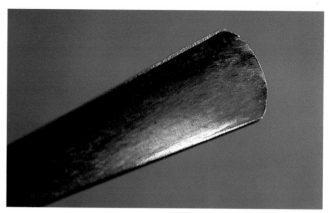

R–01
The raked-back shoulder on this gouge makes it ideal for rolling in scroll work.

The one that makes the most sense is that if the tool is doing the job for which it is intended, then it has the right design. Some shapes are better for some things than others. The "raked" shoulder is one of these.

The face of the tool is not flat, therefore it cannot make a flat STOP CUT unless it is rolled across its curve. It is, however, excellent for work where the tool needs to be rolled and manipulated by twisting to make scrolls and foliage. If the cutting edge of the tool is flat, the corners of it may hinder rolling of the tool for scrollwork.

RASP
See R–02.
The rasp is made from hardened steel and is used for shaping wood. There are different shapes for different applications. The teeth are quite different in shape from those on a FILE. Rasps are made in differ-

R–02
A rasp is ideal for rough shaping and creating textured surfaces.

ent grades of coarseness of the teeth. For rough shaping of large surface areas a rasp can be ideal–for objects such as rocking horses, gun stocks, and sculptures. Often sold without a handle, it is essential to add a handle to the TANG to protect the skin from being cut by holding the blade.

REALISM

See R–03.

Often a vexing question for the woodcarver is the relative importance of realism. Should the leaf have veins in it? How perfect does the face have to be? Does the bird need to have feathers all over it? These are the sorts of thing any artist is always considering. These are the design issues that form the crux of the finished creation. There are no rules, as design is the artist's prerogative. There are, however, some principles that may help make better choices:

✔ Most viewers observe broad impressions quickly and add their own level of detail, mostly subconsciously, to arrive at the acceptance or otherwise of the image

R–03
This rose mahogany (*Dysoxylum fraseranum*) lizard on a mulga (*Acacia anerua*) log does not need fine detail to be attractive.

they see. So an ABSTRACT horse is seen as a horse, and this makes the shape acceptable.

✔ If an object is very detailed, and the detail is wrong or in conflict with the viewer's ideas of what the detail should be, the carving will be seen as unsatisfactory.

✔ A carving that is neither abstract nor realistic is more acceptable to the viewer if the general characteristics of the subject are recognizable. For example, proportions that are accurate will more often than not excuse the lack of detailed decoration on them. The viewer will not be conscious they are missing. So a fish without scales is perfectly acceptable to the majority of viewers if the shape of the fish is

correct. But if the scales are present and they are wrong, the art will lose credibility. In Illustration R–03 the lizard is quite acceptable as a lizard because the general proportions make it perfectly recognizable. The addition of scales is irrelevant, and would most likely "spoil" it.

REFLECTED LIGHT

Reflected LIGHT is of course what makes objects visible to the human eye. The manner in which light is reflected creates the impressions that we see, and it is the interpretation of these impressions that guides our thinking. The interpretation of photographs, for example, becomes critical if these are the design inputs for a carving. Depth and shape are two of the areas that we often misinterpret from photographs, because the photograph lacks depth of field and often creates the impression that a subject is flat when it is really round. If the photographic system can't interpret reflected light satisfactorily, then it will send the wrong visual signals to the eye.

R–04
This is a medium-relief carving in Canadian birch (*Betula pubescens*), the design adapted from the first-known printed playing cards in Provence in France, circa 1440.

RESIN

A resin is an organic substance exuded from plants and trees. It may also be prepared synthetically. Distilled resin from certain species of pine tree is also known as rosin. It is used as a main ingredient in POLISH. It dries hard and shiny in its pure form, not unlike shellac. It is heat soluble, and the solvent GUM TURPENTINE is used with it for polishes. It is water resistant, and may be coated on carving tools to help prevent RUST.

In some carving situations resin in a thick "gluey" form (partially dissolved in gum turpentine) may be used to repair carvings where the color is a match with the wood. Fill the damage and let it dry, and polish as per "normal."

REVERSE BENT

A reverse bent gouge is a useful tool in special circumstances. It is the same as the BACK BENT gouge.

RIFFLER FILE

See R–05.
A riffler file is a double-ended RASP with curved ends and a variety of grades of cutting teeth. The cutting ends are about 2 inches (50 mm) long, and the overall length varies but is generally about 6 inches (150 mm). The riffler file is used for shaping where a chisel is inappropriate or cannot reach. Experiment first before applying the riffler to the wood, particularly

RELIEF CARVING

See R–04.
A relief carving is one in which the figures and forms project from the surface so that they stand wholly or partly free. There are generally three degrees of relief, any of which may be PIERCED:

✔ High relief is that where the form of the object stands above the background to a depth of at least one half its apparent circumference.

✔ Low relief is where the form is raised from the background in such a way that no part of it is entirely detached from it—such as a coin.

✔ Middle relief is between the first two.

R–05
The riffler file will tear at timber and make a similar surface texture to the rasp.

in inaccessible areas, as it may leave a surface texture that is too rough or otherwise scratched. A variety of shapes and grades are ideal for the workshop.

RIPSAW

See R–06.

A ripsaw is designed to cut ALONG THE GRAIN (meaning down the length of a board), as opposed to a CROSS-CUT saw (meaning across the board). The teeth configuration for a ripsaw is such that it is more "chisel-like" in its cutting action than the

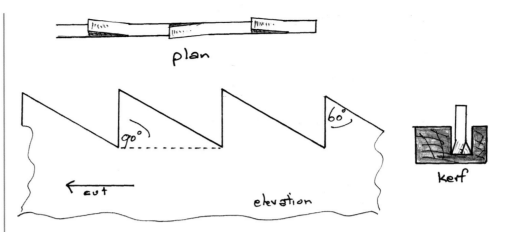

plan

90°   60°

cut   elevation   kerf

R–06

A ripsaw is not a common purchase for a woodcarver. It has a tooth configuration different from a crosscut saw.

crosscut, which tends to tear through the grain. Commonly, when a "saw" is purchased it is

the crosscut, type, the ripsaw normally having to be specified. A band saw or an electrically

powered circular saw is used mainly for ripping down lengths of timber, so unless a specific need arises for a hand-held ripsaw, it is an unlikely purchase by the woodcarver for preparing timber.

ROSETTE

See R–07.

The rosette is a common pattern in woodcarving, and derives from architecture. In architecture it is a floral design that is usually circular and has petals and/or leaves radiating symmetrically from the center. Rosettes are often incorporated in furniture designs and wall panels, and can often be seen in MISERICORDS.

R–07

Although a rosette is usually circular, the motif shown in this illustration is an Art Nouveau version of a Byzantine-style rosette, from the Roman period around AD 450. (*See also C–13.*)

R–08
Rotary burrs like this are not unlike the tools used by the dentist for grinding teeth. They may be particularly useful for carvers who cannot sustain activity with chisels.

ROTARY BURR

See R–08.
Mechanical cutting burrs are normally hand-held low-voltage appliances. They are variable speed and have a large variety of shaped cutting bits. They are very useful for shaping in awkward places, and for creating fine detail in wood that is prone to splitting or chipping with hand chisels. Noise, dust, and vibration are the downsides of their use. It may be necessary to wear earplugs, especially if burrs are run constantly at high speed; and a dust mask is a normal precaution.

ROUGHING OUT

See the letter U.
Roughing out is the term used for establishing the rough shape of a carving.

ROUTER

See R–09.
The woodcarver does not use a hand router very often. In some cases where there is a large amount of waste to be removed in the ROUGHING OUT or GROUNDING IN phase, an eletric-powered router may be ideal. Before power routers were available, hand routers had an application for clearing waste. The use of a power router may require the making of a guide jig for each job. General-purpose router tables are manufactured, and these should be studied. Power routers make considerable noise, are particularly dangerous if misused, and produce considerable dust. Comprehensive safety precautions need to be taken.

ROTARY CUTTERS

See R–10.
High-speed rotary cutters, used as attachments to hand-held angle-grinding power tools, are very useful for fast removal of substantial amounts of waste. This may be necessary for a rocking horse, for example, or for a large sculpture or a bowl. They will produce a considerable amount of noise and waste material. Protective clothing must be worn including face shield, eye goggles, and earmuffs. They require user strength for efficient use, and good control skills to ensure considerable damage is not done to the timber.

R–09
This is a hand router that can be used for the removal of background waste. The cutting knife (in the center) can be depth adjusted.

R–10
Be absolutely certain to follow all manufacturer's safety instructions with tools like this rotary cutter, and ensure no bystanders can be injured.

ROTTEN STONE

See R–11.

Rotten stone is biodegraded siliceous (i.e., containing silica) limestone and is an extremely fine gray powder. Wear a respirator to prevent breathing in the particles. It is used as a polish. For extremely fine polishing of carving tools, it can be used on a leather STROP. For carvings with a polyurethane surface finish, rub gently with rotten stone on a leather pad, plus water as a lubricant, and a fine smooth surface will be achieved. Lightly wax this surface with a wax that contains CARNAUBA, and a natural-looking finish is the result.

RPM

The standard abbreviation for "revolutions per minute," RPM is commonly used when referring to the rotation speed of electric motors. For carving, it will be used in the context of rotary cutters and hand-held rotary burrs. Higher speeds on such tools may cause burning of the wood, and lower speeds may be ineffective for cutting purposes. There is no generic "optimum" as each species will have different density and texture, and these are the main characteristics that affect the choice of speed. It is important to ensure that there is a reasonable variable speed range in the tool's specification. Also of importance is the torque, or "power output," of the tool. Ensure (by testing if possible) the tool has sufficient power at lower RPM to cut both softer and harder woods.

R–11
Rotten stone is an extremely fine abrasive. Avoid breathing in the dust.

RUST

Rust is one of the most damaging phenomena of poorly maintained tools. Rust is the OXIDATION of iron and is introduced by water. Moisture may be present in the storage environment of the tools, or the result of high humidity, or simply the sweat from your hands. A RUST INHIBITOR will help remove this problem. Sweat is particularly "dangerous" as it is high in salt, which significantly enhances the rusting process. A rusted carving blade, especially at the "sharp end," can quickly render the tool useless, as the rust causes a PITTED SURFACE and makes it impossible to SHARPEN to a usable edge. A sachet of silica gel, a hygroscopic substance that attracts water, can be used to help keep the moisture level low in tool rolls and CHISEL CHESTS.

RUST INHIBITOR

Smearing the carving chisel with oil or refined grease will help stop the formation of rust. A homemade rust inhibitor can be fashioned from RESIN, GUM

TURPENTINE, and lard from the supermarket. Heat half a pint of gum turpentine using a water bath to prevent fire, add a tablespoon of lard and a tablespoon of resin until they are melted through the liquid. Allow it to cool, and then wipe over the tool with a cloth. If it dries sticky, the resin is too strong for the mix, so add a little turpentine to the cold mix. This mixture should dry without being seen or felt, and will indefinitely protect the tool from rust.

SAFETY

Workshop safety is just as important for woodcarving as any other manual or mechanical activity. Here is a checklist to apply to your work area. It is not exhaustive; however, it contains the most common deficiencies in a woodcarving workshop:

✔ All electrical wiring in safe condition

✔ A dry floor, also free of anything that can be tripped over

✔ All flammable substances correctly protected

✔ Tools stored so they do not fall on top of you

✔ Lighting sufficiently strong that eyesight is not strained

✔ Lighting not too strong (wattage) or too close, to reduce likelihood of high heat generation or burning

✔ Effective holding devices so that the wood being carved is always held steady on the workbench, and never in the hand

✔ Sufficient space to spread out carving tools so that the carver doesn't bump into them, causing injury

✔ A tool roll, tray, or other device for holding tools so that they are not left lying all over the work area

✔ A medical emergency phone number and a first-aid kit in case of severe injury. Such injuries are normally only ever

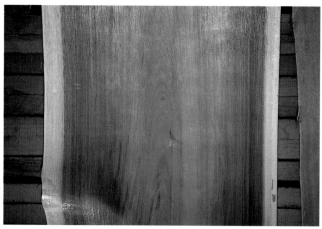

S–01

The sapwood in this slice of Tasmanian blackwood (*Acacia melanoxylon*) is the lighter stripe of wood on either side. In some species, the sapwood is not so easily distinguished.

sustained by carelessness. "Accidents" are rare in woodcarving. The most common carelessness is holding the carving in one hand and the carving chisel in the other. The inevitable slip and slice is almost guaranteed to happen, and severe injury to muscle or tendon tissue can result. Always use a HOLDING DEVICE for the carving.

SANDPAPER

Sand has in the past been used for "sandpaper"; however, a modern ABRASIVE such as ALUMINUM OXIDE or SILICON CARBIDE is now commonly used for smoothing surfaces.

SAPWOOD

See S–01.

Sapwood is the outer layer of wood underneath the bark. Sapwood is often a lighter color than the remainder, which forms the HEARTWOOD. For the carver, there is another difference that requires consideration. Sapwood is younger than the heartwood, and as a result of this it often has a different density and GRAIN characteristics. It is often more open-grained than heartwood, and may not sustain detail in the same manner. It may not hold together as well, and may be "pulpy" and crumble or break.

SAW

There are a great number of different saw types, both mechanical and hand operated. Most woodcarvers will need a range of basic saws, as follows:

✔ A BAND SAW for preparation of large blocks

✔ A CROSSCUT saw for cutting boards to length (also known as "docking")

✔ A SCROLL SAW for cutting profiles up to about 2 inches (51mm) thick, also for PIERCED RELIEF

✔ A COPING SAW as a substitute for a scroll saw

SCORP

See S–02.
The scorp is an ideal tool for some bowl-carving applications.

Coopers once used a scorp for carving the inside of wooden barrels. It is flat on the outside rim with a bevel on the inside. Care needs to be taken sharpening this tool, which requires a cylindrical SLIP STONE. LONG BENT and SHORT BENT gouges should also be considered for bowl carving, and in many cases may be more appropriate.

SCRAPER

See S–03.
The concept of the cabinetmaker's scraper is a very useful one for the woodcarver. There are many situations where scraping the surface is the most satisfactory way to clean it and finely shape it. For preparation of a flat surface to be carved, the

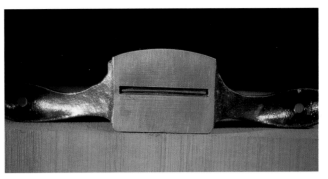

S–03
This cabinet scraper is fitted in a handle like a spokeshave. A scraper can also be made from a knife.

cabinet scraper often offers the best finish. Sanding is not ideal at all, as any residual abrasive particles will cause considerable damage to chisels, and sanding tends to "round" the surface. The scraper cuts the grain cleanly and makes a very flat, uniform surface. For smaller projecting areas of the carving itself, the cabinet scraper is of course too large; however, a top-quality KNIFE with a very hard blade can be made into a very effective scraper for these awkward surfaces. Sharpen it in the same way as for the regular scraper. Ensure the edge of the blade is perfectly flat, meaning that it is blunt, and then roll a burr on it with a BURNISHER.

SCRATCHING

See S–04.
Poorly honed carving tools cause a form of scratching not often noticed. The scratch is not noticed because the carver is using inadequate lighting, or isn't closely observing the carved surface. Any

S–04
Ensure workshop lighting is adequate, otherwise scratching from a damaged tool may not be noticed.

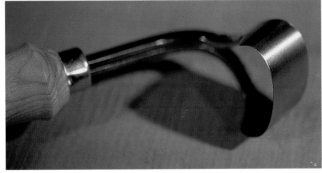

S–02
Storing a scorp needs care, as it is easy for such an "odd" shape to be damaged.

slight irregularity in the sharpened edge of a tool will be transferred to the carving in the form of minute "ridges," and will appear across the surface. If carving is continued, a fairly sizable cleanup job may be required to restore the surface to a high quality.

SCRATCH STOCK

See S–05 and S–06.
A scratch stock is essentially a miniature molding device for shaping or marking. It is relatively easy to make your own scratch stock from a small piece of wood with a hole through it to take a long, thin piece of tool steel—taken from a bro-

S–05
This scratch stock has adjustable blade depth as well as an adjustable fence for accurate work.

ken chisel or HACK-SAW blade, for example. A scratch stock can also be used for making long grooves on borders where it is too difficult to hold a gouge or "V" tool steady for long-length cuts.

SCRIBING BLOCK

See S–07.
Used for transferring height measurements from one object to another, a scribing block will normally have an arm with height and length adjustment. It is a common measuring accessory in wood

SCULPTURE, and is very useful for quick and accurate copying. Releasing a single wing nut on the model illustrated allows the adjustments to be made. The horizontal arm can reach into areas where a standard rule cannot be used.

S–06
Different-shaped blades can easily be ground, this one for making a continuous bead.

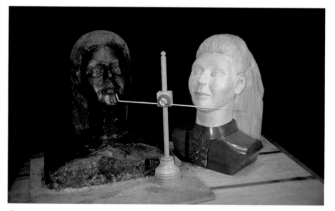

S–07
The scribing block in the center of this illustration is the easiest way to accurately transfer height measurements from the wax model to the woodcarving.

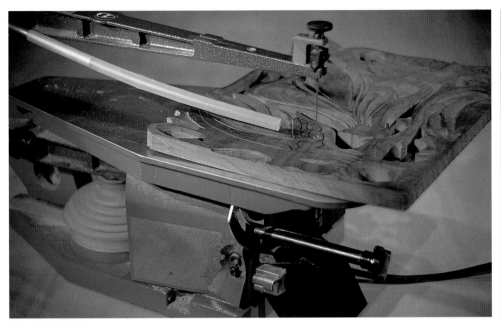

S–08
A well-manufactured scroll saw is essential for fast and accurate cutting. If the blade is blunt, a scroll saw will not cut vertically in a straight line, but in a curve, and burning may also occur.

SCROLL SAW
See S–08.
A scroll saw is a most useful power tool for the carver., used for cutting a PROFILE, and for PIERCED RELIEF pattern cutting. A wide variety of cutting blades are available for these tools, varying in both width and tooth configuration. For cutting plastics and some metals, it may be necessary to run the machine at low speeds, and therefore a variable-speed accessory is required. Consideration will need to be given to the thickness of cut and the length of cut for the majority of work to be undertaken, as the capacity of the machine is limited by these specifications.

SCULPTURE
See S–09.
A sculpture is a shape carved from a medium such as wood, stone, or wax, and is designed to represent a real or imaginary object. As such, the word is used to describe many and varied creations. It is a very loosely used word, to the point where it may really have no meaning other than the act of doing "carving." Some artists would prefer "a sculpture" to be only creations in the realm of the imaginary or abstract, rather than reality. Whatever the chosen definition, it is the creation of art, and the sculpting of form, that captures the imagination and gives "sculpture" its mystery and magic.

SEALER
Sealers are used to fill the pores of wood to create either a non-porous surface to enable further finishing work such as waxing, or to help prevent the moisture transfer to or from the atmosphere. A sealer will be an integral part of the chosen finishing technique. It may be a synthetic compound, or natural, such as SHELLAC. Sealing the

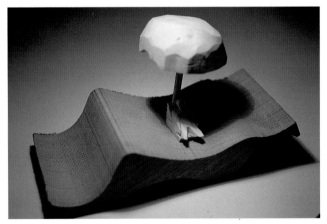

S–09
This sculpture is called *My Dad at the Beach*, and was made from workshop offcuts by John Wigham (10 years old).

surface prevents absorption of the next layer of the finish, such as a stain, from penetrating the wood. If WET WOOD is being carved, it is a good idea to reseal the surface after working the carving, using a sealing wax, and carving it off at the next session. As the wood is carved it will gradually dry, and if care is taken with storage, no CHECKING should occur during SEASONING.

SEASONING

Seasoning wood is the process by which natural water content is reduced to that of a stable relationship with the atmosphere in which it exists. Seasoning may take place artificially in a KILN, or it may be naturally air-dried. If water reduction takes place too quickly, the cell walls are likely to collapse, causing the wood to CHECK. Moisture content is measured as the ratio of the weight of the water in the wood to the weight of the wood when it is completely dry. Wood can be carved wet, and in some species it is the only way to easily carve it (such as gidgee), for it becomes too hard when it is dry. It may be necessary to use a SEALER between carving sessions. Always store a wet woodcarving out of wind and in a cool place. If a damp environment is needed to assist in a specially slow drying process, try leaving it in the bathroom, or cover it with a damp cloth.

SECONDARY BEVEL

See S–10.
The BEVEL shape on the carving tool is critical to its performance. A secondary bevel is ground on to the tool in cases where extra strength is needed so that it can cut in hard wood. The secondary bevel is normally applied to the inside of the tool. If it is applied to the outside of the tool, it alters the angle of approach of the tool into the timber. It raises it, and this makes the tool harder to use, except in cases of a steep-sided dish or bowl where a higher approach is an advantage. A secondary bevel increases the thickness of the steel at the cutting edge, making the tool stronger and less likely to SERRATE.

SERRATE

See S–11.
Serration is caused by insufficient strength in the cutting edge of the tool for the timber being carved, or by the tool banging against another tool or a hard surface. Harder woods need to be approached with care, and may require a change in the brand of tool being used and/or an alteration in the BEVEL shape, and possibly the inclusion of a SECONDARY BEVEL. Tool steel in modern chisels is an ALLOY of different hardening ingredients, and it may be that the tool being used is made from an alloy that is too brittle for hard

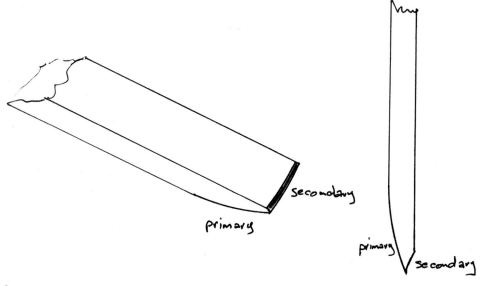

S–10
Do not automatically accept the manufacturer's bevel shape. Some experimentation may be needed to achieve optimum tool performance.

wood, particularly if the bevel is ground very thin. On the other hand, the tool steel may be too soft or weak to withstand the impact of a MALLET with hard wood. If serration occurs, there are four alternatives to review, in the order given:

1. Check for a thin bevel and regrind on a GRINDING WHEEL to make a shorter (thicker) bevel.
2. Grind a SECONDARY BEVEL on the inside of the tool.
3. If serration still occurs, the tool steel is probably too weak—change brand to a higher-density tool steel.
4. If serration still occurs, repeat 1 and 2, and if serration still occurs, the tool steel is probably too brittle. Change to a slightly less brittle tool.

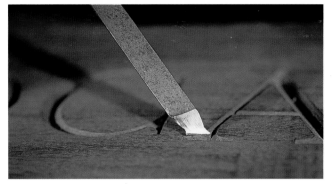

S–12
This serif spade is "homemade" from a standard skew chisel.

SERIF SPADE

See S–12.
This tool is specifically made for cutting serifs on incised lettering. The edges of the shaft are cut away to increase visibility and make it easier to cut cleanly to the bottom of the pockets that make the serif. If specialist tools such as these cannot be readily purchased, they can be made from other tools or pieces of tool steel.

Some experimentation will be necessary, and with patience some very interesting and useful tools can be homemade.

SETTING IN

See the letter U.

SHADOW

See S–13.
Shadow is the most important ingredient for carving after tools and

timber. It is by virtue of LIGHT, and the creation of shadow, that we see the shapes we carve. It is the creation of shadow that causes the illusion of depth, and allows the imagination to see perspective. Shadow is made by CROSS LIGHT, which naturally travels in straight lines, touching a ridge or edge of a carving and making it visible, while the remainder stays in darkness. Strong shadow will make visible the smallest of detail, and lack of it will allow the same detail to disappear. LIGHTING is therefore a critical tool of the woodcarver. For relief carving the shapes and definition of the formed shadows will "make or break" the success of the work.

S–11
Serration may be caused by a number of variables, including tools banging together on the workbench.

S–13
It is imperative that carving be done in a lighting environment where shadows are easily created.

S–14
The shaft of the carving chisel will break under incorrect stress, especially if it is "levered" when it becomes stuck in wood.

SHAFT

See S–14.
The shaft of some wood-carving tools is comparatively thin and therefore prone to breaking or bending. For tools such as the FISHTAIL in S–14, the shaft is narrow and can easily break or bend if mistreated. These sorts of tool are for finer finishing work and are not generally designed for heavy use. Should the tool become stuck in the wood, do not lever it back and forth to release it—the risk of breaking is too high. Carefully push the tool sideways and it will safely fall out of the wood.

SHARPENING

Sharpening is the process of refining the shape of a tool with a GRINDING WHEEL and a SLIP STONE before HONING with a STROP.

SHORT BENT GOUGE

A short bent gouge is the same as the front bent or SPOON BIT gouge.

SHORT BEVEL

See S–15.
A shorter BEVEL increases the angle of approach of the tool into the wood, and also increases the tool strength at the cutting edge. Short bevels can be difficult to work with as a result of this increase in the angle of approach; however, if a variety of densities of wood are to be carved, then it may be wise to practice with this configuration until it becomes "comfortable." Alternatively, for some of the favorite tools, it may be worth investing in a duplicate and grinding its bevels short and long. Maintaining the sharpness of a short-beveled tool is more difficult than for longer bevels, because there is a tendency to round off the cutting edge when using the STROP. A short bevel, particularly if it is slightly convex, is already heading in the direction of being rounder, and inaccurate stropping will accentuate the curve and may blunt the tool.

SILICON CARBIDE

See S–16.
Silicon carbide is an abrasive for metal. It is a gray powder and is manufactured in several grades from coarse to very, very fine. It is an excellent material for polishing wood-carving tools, especially when used with a STROP. Care should be taken using the powder, as it is very fine and can be breathed in accidentally. Always wash your hands after touching it, and never allow it near eyeglasses as it will cause significant scratching. For use on a strop, a 1000-grain size is ideal for high polishing, and for general cutting a 300-grain size is acceptable.

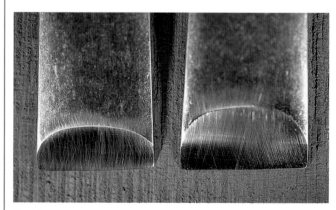

S–15
The short bevel on the left-hand tool is approximately ¼ inch (6mm) long. A longer bevel will make a thinner and finer cutting edge.

S–16
Silicon carbide is also used on "wet & dry" sandpaper, which uses water as a lubricant.

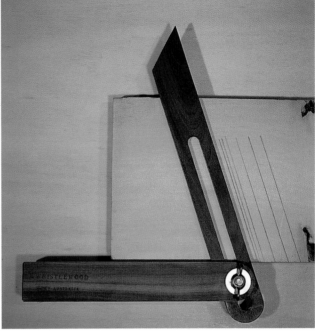

S–18
This is a handmade sliding bevel, using a very dense acacia known as gidgee (*Acacia cambegei*).

SKEW

See S–17.
The straight skew is the most effective tool for creating any shape of convex curve. It may also be useful as a KNIFE, and for gaining access into tight corners. It has a BEVEL on each side, and the angle of the cutting face to the shaft will depend on the personal preferences of the user; however, anything in the vicinity of 45 degrees is a good starting point. A bevel that is too convex makes the tool difficult to use as it will slide off convex curves, and a HOLLOW GROUND bevel may dig in too much. For the skew, a flat bevel is possibly the best. Use the skew in a PARING action, the hand nearest the carving pushing or pulling, and the other hand on the handle steadying it. A SPOON BENT SKEW is very useful for INCISED lettering.

SLICING

A slicing cutting action is the same as PARING.

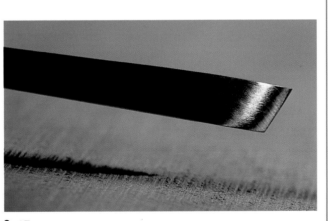

S–17
The skew chisel is the simplest yet possibly the most versatile of all carving tools.

SLIDING BEVEL

See S–18.
A sliding bevel is used primarily by carpenters and cabinetmakers for transferring angles and for marking out repeated angles. A woodcarver will not use it very frequently; however, it is useful to have in the TOOL KIT. Sometimes it is handy for quick reference when comparing an original drawing to the carving or for checking accuracy of miters on picture frames. There may also be occasions when a panel needs to be adjusted to fit an existing opening, and an angle needs to be assessed and transferred to new work.

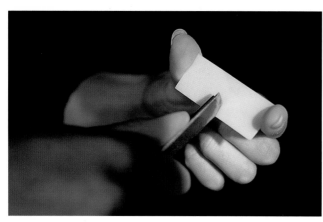

S–19
Hold the slip stone between the thumb and index finger, and for best control rotate the stone around the tool.

SLIP STONE

See S–19.

A slip stone is used for the SHARPENING process. Once the tool has been ground to the required basic shape on a GRINDING WHEEL, it is then further refined on a slip stone. This second stage is called sharpening, and following this is the process of HONING on a STROP. In many woodwork workshops there is a BENCH STONE, which is by and large inappropriate for sharpening woodcarving tools. A bench stone is used on a bench for sharpening tools with constant bevel angles, such as plane blades. Woodcarving tools, for the most part, have a curved CROSS SECTION and often a CONVEX bevel. As they are comparatively small tools and comprise these compound curves, it is important to be able to see what is happening during the sharpening activity. A bench stone does not allow this; a small slip stone does. Lubricate the slip stone with NEATSFOOT OIL for best results.

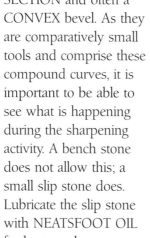

S–20
This short-shafted spade gouge fits snugly in the hand for fine smoothing work.

SMOOTH CUT

A smooth cut should be the aim of every wood-carver! Unfortunately, unless some key elements are in balance, it will not be possible. These are:

✔ The tool must be finely HONED.

✔ The BEVEL must be appropriate for the timber.

✔ The wood being carved must be firmly fixed by a HOLDING DEVICE for the work surface.

✔ A steady stroke of the tool must be achieved, not a series of little JERKY CUTS.

✔ If a MALLET is used, it should not be underweight or over-weight for the work it has to do.

✔ The cutting direction must not be AGAINST THE GRAIN.

SOUND

Sound is, on first consideration, an unlikely carving partner. However, sound has one very particular and very useful purpose. Sound can be used to assess the sharpness of your tools. A sharp tool will create a sound with wood that is quite different from a blunt tool. Each species will be slightly different; however, a sharp tool will make a clean, swishing (almost whistling) sound as it cuts across the wood, and a blunt tool will make a dull grating sound as it tears the surface. Try different woods with sharp and blunt tools, and select one that creates a distinctive sound and use it as a standard test for sharpness.

SPADE GOUGE

See S–20.

The spade gouge is usually a light-finishing tool. The protruding shoulders make it very useful for accessing tight spots and narrow grooves and corners. This shape of tool is excellent for cutting INCISED LETTERING and for smoothing large expanses.

SPECIES

The different trees that wood comes from have characteristics assigned to them that enable them to stand alone as a unique specimen or be grouped together as specimens with common features. These classifications of individual or group characteristics are then assigned a name, which may be derived from the person who assigned the characteristics or by other means. These classifications are called species, and the assigned name is the way the species is identified, and is called its BOTANICAL NAME. Trees also have COMMON NAMES that are used for reference in "nonbotanical" terms. "Douglas Fir" is the common name for the species with the botanical name *Pseudotsuga menziesii.* Classification of a species is arrived at by the study of a large number of characteristics, some of them being the shape of the leaf, the color of the bark, the nature of the seed, and the color and shape of the flower.

SPLITTING

See S–21.
This is damage done when a tool is forced into wood and the wood breaks apart. The end result is similar to CHECKING, which is a natural occurrence of CELLS shrinking as

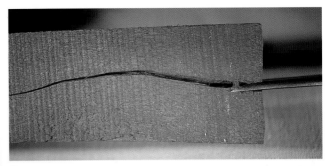

S–21
Splitting is likely to occur when the expectation is to cut too much away in one attempt.

they dry out during the SEASONING process. Splitting during the carving process is the result of poor technique. It may be that the tool is pushed into the wood AGAINST THE GRAIN, or the carver is trying to remove too much wood at once. The tool may be too large for the task, it may be blunt and not capable of cutting cleanly, or the chosen wood may not be suitable for carving at all. Open- or coarse-grain wood is more prone to splitting during carving than fine close-grain wood.

SPOKESHAVE

See S–22.
The spokeshave is, as the name implies, designed for the carving of wheel spokes. However, it may be used wherever there is a need to cut corners or edges that cannot be effectively cut with a chisel or gouge. There are different kinds of spokeshave, flat on the sole, or convex, or concave. The most common is flat. The cutting blade is similar to a carpenter's hand plane, and is sharpened the same way.

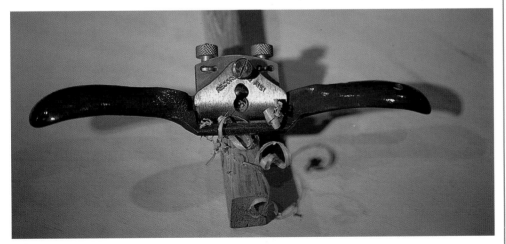

S–22
Use the spokeshave by either pulling towards the body or pushing away, whichever gives the greater control. A spokeshave can be used for making carved walking sticks.

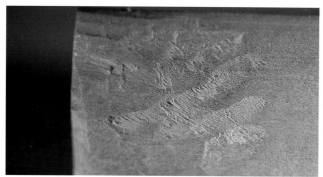

S–23
This is Australian kauri (*Agathis microstachya*), and it can be spongy, causing a torn look unless the tool is very finely honed.

SPONGY WOOD

See S–23.
Some SPECIES of wood are quite "spongy" under a chisel. A tool with a very finely honed thin BEVEL is best for cutting such wood. It is advisable to test a timber with some chisel strokes before embarking on the carving project, to ensure the wood is suitable for the intended purpose. It may be necessary to regrind some tools to allow them to perform. In many cases, commercially available wood that is suitable for machining such as with a lathe or spindle molder is unsuitable for carving.

SPONTANEOUS COMBUSTION

Spontaneous combustion is an often forgotten workshop hazard, and may cause fire damage. It may occur given the right temperature conditions in old rags full of organic OILS such as LINSEED and TUNG. It is important to remove these rags from enclosed spaces once they have been used and dispose of them in a safe manner. Washing before throwing away with household rubbish is a most effective disposal method.

SPOON-BIT GOUGE

See S–24.
A spoon-bit gouge is another name for short bent gouge. They are designed to allow access for cutting tight curves and very deep recesses. When SHARPENING these tools, it is important to follow the flow of the curve of the spoon

S–24
Ensure that the angle of the bevel of the spoon-bit gouge allows the tool to be easily used around sweeping curves.

when shaping the BEVEL. Grinding too acute a bevel on the cutting edge of the blade will make the angle of approach of the tool into the wood so high (or even tipping over) as to be almost impossible to use. These tools will not normally be used with a MALLET, as the curvature of the cut makes it too difficult; however, this does not mean they should not be tried.

SPOON-BIT SKEW

See S–25.
This tool is handled in a similar way to the straight SKEW; however, its bent blade makes it suitable for cutting concave curves as opposed

S–25
Ensure that the angle of the bevel of the spoon-bit skew encourages smooth and easy use. Too acute an angle may make this tool hard to use.

to convex as with the straight skew. It is notably useful for the faces of INCISED LETTERING and hollow-molding the corners of borders. Use it for foliage and scrolls and similar applications. Spoon-bit skews are manufactured in left- and right-handed versions, and there is a bevel on one side only, unlike the straight skew, which is double sided.

STAIN

Stains may occur naturally in wood, as the result of such things as RESINS, mold or fungus growth, or introduced metals such as iron from nails and screws. Stains may also be introduced as PIGMENTS in wood-coloring surface finishes. Naturally occurring stains may sometimes be removed by bleaching, or simply left as an integral feature of the work. If the carving is to be artificially stained to alter its color, be sure the color is as required by testing on an offcut first. On a sample try a SEALER, which will reduce or stop penetration of the stain into the timber, and an unsealed sample, which will allow

penetration and impart quite a different "look" to the wood.

STEEL

Woodcarving tools are made from steel, and each manufacturer has its own particular "blend." Modern tools are often an ALLOY using ingredients such as chrome vanadium. Alloyed materials that are hard tend to hold their sharp edge longer than those that are not; however, they are also often more brittle, and therefore easier to damage and harder to repair. Such tools are often inappropriate for harder woods, whereas a softer steel will not chip or serrate as easily and can be

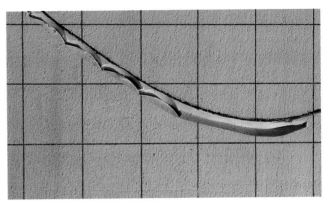

S–26
The stop cut is the first vertical cut. In this illustration it is the "scallop"-shaped set of incisions along a groove made by a "V" tool.

kept sharp with less effort. As tools age, the steel often crystallizes and becomes brittle and crumbly. Antique tools are not necessarily a good buy for this reason. As collector's items yes, but as workshop tools they are suspect.

S–27
Once the stop cut is in place, make a slicing cut along the surface to be removed, so that it meets the stop cut and the waste falls out.

STOP CUT

See S–26 and S–27, and the letter U.

The stop cut is one of the most important carving cuts. It is relevant mostly to RELIEF CARVING; however, in some situations with CARVING IN THE ROUND it also occurs. The stop cut is the vertical incision that commences the waste removal during SETTING IN, and it is used continuously as a technique throughout the carving process. Once the vertical cut is in place, a slicing cut is made along the grain up to the bottom of the stop cut. If the stop cut and the slicing cut meet cleanly together, the waste that is created will come away easily. If not, re-cut until it does, and do not twist the tool in an effort to get it to come out; also, don't flick or pull at the waste with the fingers. Either of these might damage either the tool SHAFT or the carving.

STRAIGHT CHISEL

See S–28 and S–29.
The straight chisel is the carver's equivalent of the carpenter's FIRMER chisel. It has a BEVEL on both sides for convenience. This tool is used for any straight-line cutting, cleaning corners (a MACARONI might be a better choice), and can substitute for a SKEW, although not very successfully.

S–28
The carpenter's straight chisel on the left may be substituted for the carver's straight chisel on the right—however, with limited success.

S–29
The double-sided bevel of the carver's straight chisel allows it to be easily used left- and right-handed, and is more convenient for shaping convex curves.

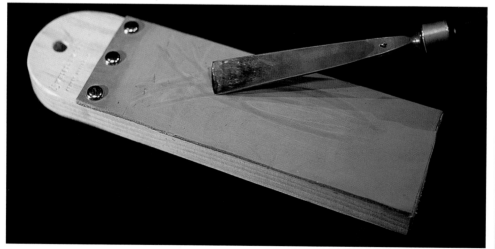

S–30
Dress the strop with silicon carbide or aluminum oxide powder to enhance the polishing process.

STRINGY

Stringy or WOOLLY is a description often given to wood grain that is characterized by long fibers that won't easily cut off. SPLITTING wood is sometimes also stringy. Such woods are unsuitable for carvings that require fine detail, and are better suited to larger, chunkier SCULPTURE. To successfully carve a stringy timber, apart from choosing an appropriate design, tools must be sharp and the BEVEL thin and long.

STROP

See S–30.
The strop is used for HONING the tools after SHARPENING. This activity is extremely important, as it is the process that polishes the BEVEL. It removes all the scratches that have been put there by the GRINDING wheel and the SLIP STONE. It is also the process that maintains a fine edge during the carving activity, between those times when the slip stone and grinder may be needed. Do not hold the tool at an angle higher than the bevel angle, otherwise the sharp edge will be

rounded off and made blunt. Only use hard belly-hide LEATHER.

STROPPING PASTE

Stropping pastes are added to the surface of the leather STROP to increase the abrasivity and enhance the polishing process. If a specific stropping paste cannot be found, try toothpaste, chrome polish, jeweler's rouge, brass polish, fine pumice, rotten stone, aluminum oxide, or silicon carbide at around 1000 grain, or engine valve-grinding paste. The paste will discolor as it collects steel particles from the carving tool, and it will eventually clog the pores of the leather with these parti-

cles, in which case the cutting action of the strop will be significantly reduced. Scrape the surface of the leather to clean it, or replace it altogether.

SUPERFOOT

A superfoot is a standard cubic measure of timber, and is 144 cubic inches. A block measuring 6 inches × 6 inches × 6 inches is 1½ superfeet.

SWEEP

See S–31.
The sweep of the carving tool is the profile or CROSS SECTION of the cutting edge of the tool. Manufacturer's catalogs show their tool shapes by using profile sets.

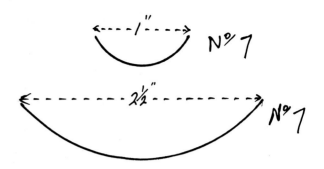

S–31
The size of the sweep of the tool is measured in a straight line shoulder to shoulder, and the arc is usually designated by a number.

Today's manufacturers also used numbering systems to identify the tools in their ranges, and these numbers generally have little or no relationship between manufacturers. In historical times, there were geographic regional sets of patterns that manufacturers used, so there was similarity

between brands. Note that each sweep under the same number is not just a wider version of the same curve. It is part of the ARC from parallel curves emanating from the same center.

SYMMETRY

See S–32.
Symmetry is sought in architectural carving where one side of the work needs to be the same as the other. In nature subjects, however, symmetry is rare, and should only be applied if it actually exists, otherwise the subject will look "unreal." The human eye registers asymmetry, and the brain interprets it and often "removes" it from the vision. Most nature subjects "look" even when in fact they aren't.

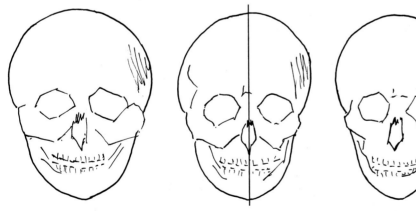

S–32
The human adult's skull shape, drawn from photographs, creates some very unrealistic images if symmetry is introduced. These are of an actual person. The center sketch is the "real" one. The left-hand sketch is the left-hand "half" duplicated, and the right-hand sketch the right-hand "half" duplicated. The carving of this person is the bust in Illustration S-07, on page 110.

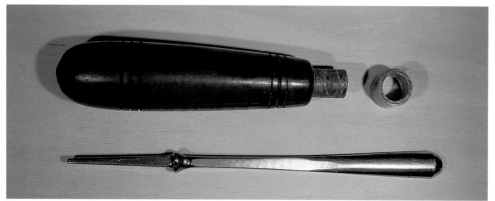

T–01
Place the ferrule on the handle before putting the handle on! An external ferrule in shown—it is the ring in the top right-hand corner.

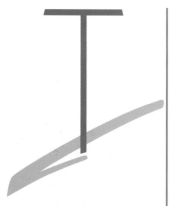

TANG

See T–01.

The tang is that part of the tool that fits up into the HANDLE. It is normally tapered and square in cross section. Sometimes the tang is misshapen and this can make it difficult to insert. If so, it is necessary to grind it to a more reasonable shape on a GRINDING WHEEL. The hole in the handle needs to approximate the shape of the tang, and a TAPERED BIT is best for drilling the hole. The hole needs to be in ALIGNMENT with the handle so the blade is not crooked. Make the hole about ¼ inch shorter than the tang, and sharpen the tang so it will penetrate the wood at the end of the hole in the handle when it is tapped home.

TAPERED BIT

See T–02 and T–03.

The tapered bit is ideal for setting the TANG into the HANDLE of the chisel. If a tapered bit is not available, drill two holes as shown in H–07 for HANDLE RE-PLACEMENT. Drill the holes slowly so as not to force the bit into the handle and split it.

T–02
This is a hand-held tapered bit. It is like a reamer. Pre-drill a smaller hole and ream to shape with the bit.

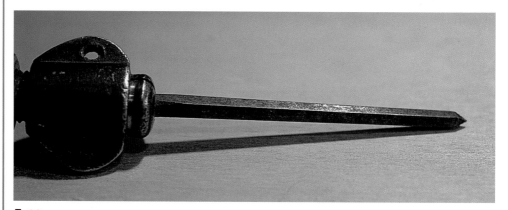

T–03
A close-up of the tapered bit, showing a four-sided cross section. Try making one if it can't be purchased.

Choose a bit of best fit for the tang, and resist the temptation to have the thicker end of the tang be the part that holds the blade in the handle—forcing a fit at this end may cause the handle to split (although there is a ferrule in place). The pointed end of the tang should penetrate the handle.

TEARING CUT

See T–04.
Tearing of the surface of the wood by the chisel is caused either by a blunt tool or by cutting AGAINST THE GRAIN. The tool may simply need a minute on the STROP to restore the cutting edge, or it may need re-SHARPENING.

Try the strop first. Sometimes a burr on the cutting edge is responsible for a torn surface. A burr may also be caused by wood, or by dropping or banging the tool against a clamp or other metal surface. It is necessary to store woodcarving tools in a TOOL ROLL or TOOL CHEST so that they cannot bang against one another and cause damage.

TEMPLATES

See T–05 and T–06.
A template is the traditional way of storing a pattern for repeated use. Make templates out of thin, stable timber such as good-quality plywood or a composite material such as

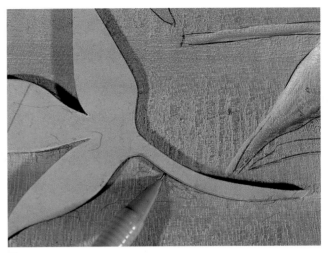

T–05
Be sure the pencil mark is as close as possible to the template corner, otherwise the tracing will be oversized.

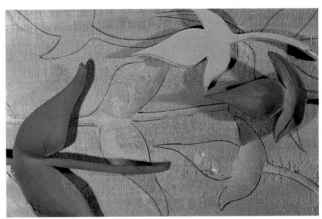

T–06
In this example of making leaves, one side of the leaf is carved after the template is traced, and before being cut out with a scroll saw or a coping saw.

T–04
This sample of Huon pine (*Dacrydium franklinii*) shows how the grain tears when cut against the grain. It is also described as "flaky."

medium-density fiberboard. When tracing around a template, ensure the pencil has a fine tip and reaches the actual junction of the edge of the pattern and the timber surface.

Holding the sharp pencil at an angle will achieve this. If it is held vertically, the edge of the pencil will rest on the edge of the template and the pattern drawn will be oversized.

T–07
A background punch has been used to add texture to hide the unevenly carved surface.

T–08
Rust, dust, and safety are three issues that may rule out an open-air tool rack.

TEXTURE

See T–07.
The final texture of the surface of the woodcarving can be an important feature of the art. Texture can add SHADOWS to the surface and improve the overall appearance. Texture may appear naturally in the grain of the wood, particularly with coarse-grained species. Texture could be made with a RASP, or marking with a GOUGE. Background PUNCHES are also used to "disguise" rough surfaces.

TOOTHPASTE

As an abrasive paste for a STROP, toothpaste is worth trying. It is readily available and relatively cheap. It must be of a formulation that contains an ABRASIVE such as calcite. Clear gel varieties generally have no or very little abrasive, and some varieties known as "smoker's" toothpaste have the highest abrasive content.

TOOL RACK

See T–08.
For the workshop, a tool rack is a useful storage system. These can be permanent like the one illustrated, or made in smaller sections and be mobile. Place the tools in the rack handle first, so that they can be easily identified. If there are small children coming into the workshop, place the rack out of their reach. Tools stored in the open air are more prone to RUST than those in a closed environment, and need to be checked frequently.

TOOL ROLL

See T–09.
For compact portability, a tool roll is an excellent storage system. The material is important, and CANVAS is ideal. Place the tools in the roll pockets, handle first, so that they can be identified easily. Over time the roll will become very soiled and probably cut by the tool ends, and will need replacing.

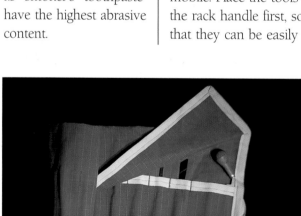

T–09
A waterproof canvas tool roll helps prevent the formation of rust.

TRY SQUARE

See T–10.

The carpenter's try square is sometimes useful for preparation of wood for carving, and for assisting with the laying out of patterns. A wooden square has the advantage that if it is accidentally dropped on the carving it is unlikely to damage the surface in the same way as a metal square. A good-quality wooden try square will remain square provided it is "looked after" and stored where it cannot get wet, overheated in the sun, or dried out by wind.

TUNG OIL

Tung oil is from the tung tree, a native of China. It is a centuries-old wood OIL finish, and may be appropriate for a carved surface where a hard, oiled look is required. Tung oil is naturally a medium-brown color slightly darker than LINSEED OIL, and it further darkens with age. It is generally applied in either its raw form or with the addition of cooked oil, which tends to make the finish more shiny. It will harden over time, and the raw oil dries

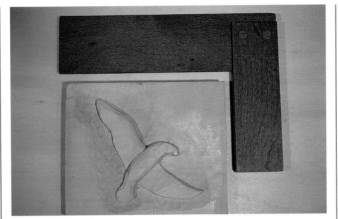

T–10
Wooden tools like try squares are not common, modern products being made from steel or plastics. This one is handmade from beefwood (*Gravillia striata*).

very slowly. Many coats may be necessary to achieve a quality finish; however, the results on carved surfaces where dark, rich color is required can be quite outstanding.

TURNING

See T–11.

Wood turning is done with a machine called a lathe, which holds the timber in place while it spins. Cutting tools called gouges are pressed into the surface to create shapes. There are different kinds of turning, such as spindle turning for making items such as candle sticks, and bowl turning for bowls, platters and the like. Turning tools are not dissimilar to carving tools, except that they are generally much larger and stronger.

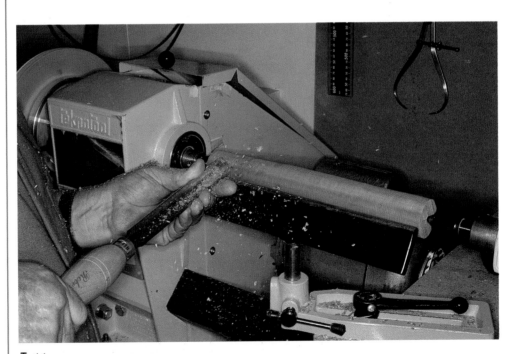

T–11
Spindle turning is being done on this lathe. The gouge being used is similar in shape to, but much larger than, a woodcarving gouge.

Understanding what to do in what order to create a successful woodcarving

*See also the letter Q —
"Answers to the twenty
most asked questions
about woodcarving"*

UNDER-STANDING RELIEF CARVING

1
Selection of design and preparation of timber

Select the design and the timber so that there is compatibility between the two in terms of size, grain density, and texture, and suitability for the final application (e.g., furniture, wall plaque, signs and so on).

The wood should be prepared with all surfaces smooth so that there is no likelihood of damaging the completed carving by planing edges after the event.

2
Transferring design to timber

See U–01.
If not drawn directly on to the wood, transferring the design is best done with CARBONIZED PAPER. Tape the drawing to be copied to the wood so it does not move. It is also a good idea to store a copy of the drawing in a safe place.

U–02

U–01

3
Mark on background depth

See U–02.
Mark the desired depth of the carving on the edge of the wood. Use a DEPTH GAUGE if this is not practical. It may be that the carving is on the center of a large board and the background will not be removed all the way to the edge.

4
Roughing out or grounding in

See U–03.
Start by incising around the outside edge of the outline with a "V" TOOL to a depth of a millimeter or two at the most. This has the effect of making the outline very visible, and of separating the surface fibers, which helps reduce CHIPPING around the edge of the carving as you progress. It also serves as a guide for the next action:

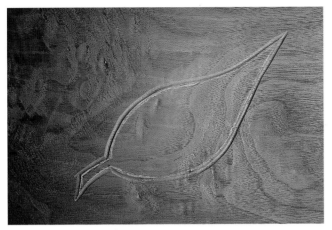

U–03

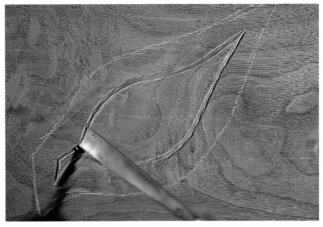

U–04

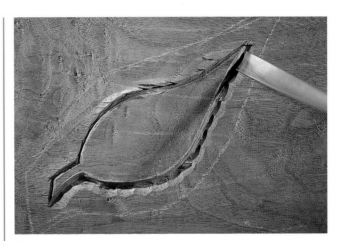

U–05

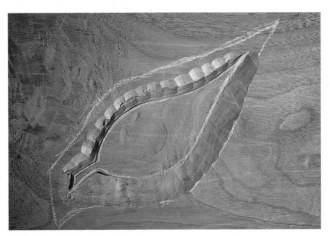

U–06

See U–04.
With a standard straight GOUGE the size depending on the size of the carving, make an incision along the "V" tool cut, using it as a guide. Place the gouge in the groove with the BEVEL towards the pattern, and if necessary with a MALLET for control and power, make a cut at an angle of about 45 degrees into the wood, in a direction away from the pattern. Cut all around the pattern in this manner.

See U–05.
Overlap each cut only a small amount, and cut to a depth of about ⅛ inch (3mm) to begin. Then, in the reverse direction, cut back towards the first cut, removing the waste.

The two cuts should meet in the middle, with the waste "popping out" easily. Do not break it out with your fingers or twist it out with the tool. Re-cut if necessary. Repeat this procedure until the desired depth is reached, using the depth gauge or the mark around the edge of the wood as the guide.

See U–06.
Gradually move farther and farther from the pattern, so that when the desired depth is reached, all the unwanted wood has been removed and the background (the "GROUND") is flat and the pattern roughly exposed ("ROUGHING OUT").

U–07

U–08

5
Setting in

See U–07.
It is important to achieve a vertical edge around the pattern, and that this edge is right on the pattern line. It will be necessary to hold the gouge so that the bevel is vertical, and this will mean the tool will lean forward at the angle of the bevel. If a vertical edge is not achieved right at the drawn line of the pattern, the carving will be "oversized."

Ensure that where the background and the edge of the pattern meet, there is a clean 90-degree junction, unless of course the pattern specifically requires otherwise.

6
Modeling, or bosting

See U–08.
Use the various tools at your disposal for the MODELING process. This is extremely interesting work, and the process by which the shapes and shadows are created. As relief carving is all about the creation of SHADOWS, every cut should be done with this in mind. Think relief, think shadow. Identify FOCAL LINES and POINTS, LAYERS, and relationships. Remember that natural subjects have no flat surfaces and that curves should be smooth and free of kinks.

7
Final setting in or cleanup

See U–09, U–10, U–11.
As the modeling process continues, it may be necessary to adjust the depth of the background when the design becomes more visible. There may also be changes to the design that become necessary when all the components of it are seen in the actual carved form.

Look at the carving from a distance. This often changes the perspective of its elements. Also alter the LIGHTING. CROSS-LIGHT it from different directions to ensure it conveys the image intended.

Make all the necessary adjustments, and finally make sure all the surfaces are clean and the texture is free from unintended damage. Use a DEPTH GAUGE to ensure accurate and uniform depth throughout the carving.

8
Undercutting

See U–12.
Undercutting around the edge about 1 to 1½ millimeters above the BACKGROUND is the final activity for the carving. With an almost flat gouge, make the first cut at a fairly steep angle downwards just above the background. Then, along the flat of the back-

U–09

U–10

ground, cut in underneath the pattern to meet the first cut. The very small amount of waste should come away easily.

This will place a shadow line underneath the carving and add strength and visibility to its outline, while at the same time "lifting" it from the background. It will increase depth illusion and enhance the carving considerably.

9
Finishing

See U–13.
Finish with an appropriate surface coating. It is important that the carving be sealed, as the wood cells will collect dust and the appearance of the carving will go a dull gray. In the illustration (U-13) there is no surface finish. The wood

U–11

U–13

U–12

is American walnut (*Juglans* spp.), which polishes to a good shine, provided it is well sealed before wax is applied. Before the finish is applied, it will be necessary to decide what to do with the textured area left by chisel cuts around the perimeter of the leaf. The internal surface area of the leaf needs smoothing, and the carver will need to decide whether or not to cut in veins. Make these decisions before applying surface finishes, as while it is not impossible to re-carve, it is more difficult, once a finish is applied, to make alterations.

UNDER-STANDING CARVING IN THE ROUND

1
Selection of design and preparation of timber

The principles of selection of wood and design are much the same as for carving in relief. It may be necessary to consider additional areas such as

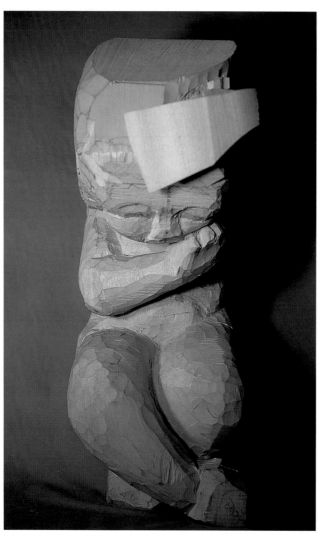

U–14

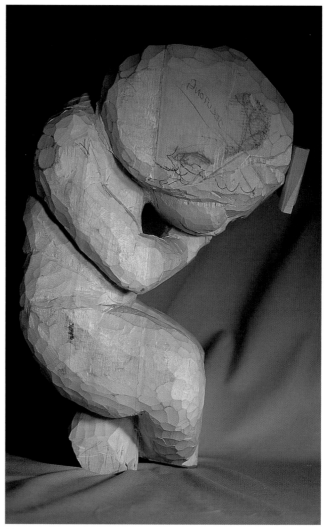

U–15

the suitability of timber for outdoor situations or the weight of the wood and subsequent stability if the carving is to be mounted on a PEDESTAL. Color will be equally important, as will GRAIN texture and figure in the wood.

2
Cutting in profiles

See U–14 and U–15.
Draw or trace on the front-to-back and side-to-side PROFILES. There is only need to draw those that have the greatest surface area. The profile front to back will be the same as the one back to front. The same applies left to right and right to left. The profiles can then be cut with a band saw or handsaw as appropriate, and this will clearly save a lot of carving time. Be careful with arms and legs—sometimes it is a bit confusing as to what the profile actually is, and it may be easier not to pre-cut the profile at all, but to carve from scratch. In the case of U–14, a carving block was LAMINATED from pieces previously roughly band-sawed to shape.

U–16

3
Modeling

The modeling process is quite different from relief carving. The three-dimensional nature requires visualization skills for proportion and interpretation of shape relationships, and these are best developed by observation and experimentation. Where there is uncertainty, WAX or other modeling media can be used for the development of ideas. DIVIDERS or COMPASS are useful for checking measurements, and cardboard TEMPLATES or a PROFILING GAUGE for matching curves one side to the other. Use a SCRIBING BLOCK for transferring heights if a model is used.

As woodcarving in the round is the process of "carving down" rather than "building up," it is very important that great care be taken not to remove too much material—it can't be put back very easily, if ever! Careful thought needs to be given to each cut of the tool. The more familiar the carver is with the subject, the better, particularly while the skills of observation and interpretation are being developed.

4
Detailing

See U–16.
The detailing process is where the fine nuances are introduced. These are the shapes that give the ultimate character to the work: a wrinkle on the skin, a twist in a petal, or a curl on a lip. As with most art forms, it is the subtlety of these expressions that makes all the difference. Such additions are also in the realm of shadow creation, just as with relief carving. Good lighting is

very important to complete this process. To help work out just what to do, simple sketches or models are particularly helpful.

5
Finishing

See U–17.
As for relief carving, sealing the surface is very important. Be careful that the chosen finish does not interfere with the subtleties that have been carved into the work. A too shiny surface may make an expressive shadow disappear. Conversely, too flat a finish, such as an application of OIL, may make a highlight too hard to see. If the surface of the timber is sealed with a clear mat product, it is most likely that any natural finish that is applied over it will be removable. A synthetic finish may react with the sealer if it too is synthetic, and may amalgamate with or alter it and be impossible to remove. U–17 shows the right foot of the cherub with a GESSO finish, ready for GILDING.

U–17

"V" TOOL
A "V" tool is the same as a PARTING TOOL.

VARNISH
Varnish is a term loosely applied to a variety of finishes whether natural or synthetic, and, like LACQUER, varnish creates a surface with considerable shine. Before applying a shiny finish to a woodcarving, particularly a finish that cannot be easily removed, it is important to consider the implications that shine will have on the work. Shine is reflected LIGHT. Shine potentially reduces shadows significantly and therefore the visibility of the shadows that have been painstakingly created. Shine can have the effect of altering shape perception (because it alters shadow relationships). Shine can simply be quite inappropriate a finish. If there is any doubt, start with a dull finish, and build up the shine. For example, use a synthetic mat, then satin or semigloss and then a high-gloss finish. Each of these can be dulled with fine abrasive and oiled for a more "natural" look if things start to look wrong. Test and experiment wherever possible.

VEGETABLE OIL
Natural OIL finishes can be achieved with household cooking oils, such as OLIVE OIL. Other oils that may be used for surface finishing are TUNG OIL and LINSEED OIL.

VEINER
See V–01.
This tool is very similar to the FLUTER but with longer sides, for making deeper recesses. There is no other difference. When SHARPENING a

V–01
The veiner may have thin sides, and special care needs to be taken during the sharpening process so that it is not damaged.

V–02

This illustration is a "mock-up" of a relief carving where the stop cut has been cleaned to a vertical edge. On the left-hand shape an undercut has been placed to show the shadow effect (indicated by the blue arrowhead), which is missing on the right-hand shape, where there is no undercut (indicated by the red arrowhead).

veiner, it is important to be careful not to over-grind the shoulders or "corners" of the cutting edge. It is very easy to remove too much steel and make the shoulders so thin they either burn and become very weak (lose their "temper") or simply break or burr over under pressure of cutting wood.

VENEER

A veneer is a thin layer of wood that is glued to a surface. Several layers glued together make PLY-WOOD. Veneer is normally approximately ¹⁄₁₆ inch thick, and is therefore quite inappropriate as a carving medium. When undertaking restoration work, ensure that areas of veneered work are clearly identified. Sometimes veneering work is so well executed that it is very difficult to distinguish between it and solid timber.

VERTICAL EDGES

See V–02.
See also under the letter U. The vertical edge around the pattern is a fundamental cut for relief carving. It is also part of the creation of

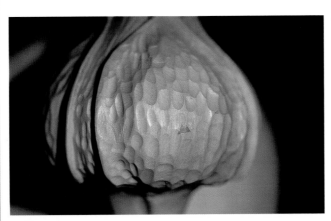

V–03

Vertical light does not allow for good shadow creation or good visibility of the carving. Turn to Illustration C–30, where the very same red arrowhead is highlighting a chip, made visible by the more effective cross lighting.

the STOP CUT. Once the gouge cuts are made vertically, it may be necessary to remove the small scallops that form on the edge between each cut. The size of these scallops will depend on the depth of the SWEEP of the tool that was used. It is best to use the flattest tool that is reasonable for these vertical stop cuts, to minimize the scallop effect and therefore minimize the cleanup. UNDERCUTTING is often done to the bottom of the vertical edge in relief carving.

VERTICAL LIGHT

See V–03.
Vertical light is a good all-round ambient LIGHT to carve by, but it is not effective for the creation of SHADOWS. The only way to ensure the lighting is effective in the workshop is to experiment with it. It is also good workshop practice to have the flexibility of different lighting arrangements. Take care when locating lights not to place them too close to the carving, otherwise they may be too hot or be broken by a mallet movement.

VISE

See V–04.

Vises are holding devises, but unlike CARVER'S SCREWS, CAMS, BENCH HOOKS, BASEBOARDS, and HOLDFASTS they hold the work between two jaws. There is an endless variety of designs for vises, and some more suitable for woodcarving than others. Whichever design is chosen, here are some key features that must be taken into consideration:

✔ The vise must be capable of being firmly fixed to a stable workbench or other workstation.

✔ The vise must be capable of withstanding the pressure and jarring effect of using a mallet without moving.

✔ The jaws of the vise must be made from or lined with a material, such as wood, that will not damage a tool if it is accidentally banged into it.

✔ The mechanics of the vise must be such that the jaws cannot open accidentally. A screw thread is the safest mechanism.

✔ The workstation must be such that the vise can be located conveniently and at the correct height for the carver. Correct height will vary from person to person; however, the top of the jaws at the height of the forearm held horizontally is a generally successful guide.

V–04
Wooden faces on the jaws of a vise help prevent damage to both the tools and the carving.

WALNUT OIL

Walnut oil was the traditional medieval wood finish. Different oils can be used as wood finishes, and another one from the kitchen is OLIVE OIL.

WARP

A warp is a distortion away from an intended shape. It may occur in wood for a number of reasons, mostly to do with the manner in which it dries during the SEASONING process. Warp may also occur if the wood is weather damaged during storage by heat or wind (which will dry it), or water (which will swell it). Warping is a generic term covering specific types such as BOWING, CUPPING, DIAMONDING, WINDING, and the CROOK and KINK.

WATER GILDING

Water gilding is the application of gold leaf to a carved surface, normally coated with GESSO, using distilled water as the carrier with the leaf adhering to the carving by the molecular attraction of the two touching surfaces. A water-gilded surface can be burnished to a bright sheen. Water gilding does not create a moisture barrier in the same way that OIL GILDING does, therefore some degrading of the carving may occur in fine joins if there is moisture gain or loss in the wood.

WATERSTONE

A waterstone is similar to a SLIP STONE or BENCH STONE except its lubricant is water, and it is normally soaked in water before use and is sometimes stored in water. Waterstones are often of exceptionally fine grain and are capable of producing a very finely honed edge.

WATER WHEEL

See W–01.
A water wheel is a style of GRINDING WHEEL used during the SHARPENING process, the water ensuring no overheating and subsequent loss of temper. A water wheel generally rotates significantly more slowly than a regular stone, and the one illustrated is geared to a ratio of about 1:20. The water wheel may be natural stone or synthetic compound, and it either rotates

W–01
It is imperative to remove the source of water from the stone when it is not in use, otherwise prolonged immersion will soften that part of the stone underwater, and it will wear more quickly in this area and the wheel become uneven.

through a water bath or has a drip feed system to deliver water to it. The water is the lubricant and helps keep the stone washed clean of tool filings.

WAX

Wax is used as a MODELING medium. There are different commercially available modeling waxes, with different melting points. A good wax for a carving model, sometimes known as a MAQUETTE, is one that softens in the hands or if placed in hot water.

A wax is a good choice for modeling as it is firm, stores easily without degrading,

and can be re-used many times. The model of the bust in S–07 (SCRIBING BLOCK) is made from wax.

WET & DRY PAPER

See W–02.
Wet & dry sanding paper is an ABRASIVE such as SILICON CARBIDE on a paper or cloth backing that is waterproof. Water is used as the lubricant, to keep the paper backing from being clogged with wood particles. This form of abrasive paper would not usually be used directly on raw timber, but on a finish such as a polyurethane coating. Continuous washing of the paper in water will keep it clean.

W–02
Wet & dry paper is an excellent last sanding medium before waxing on a surface that has been sealed.

W–03
This illustration is the carver's whittling knife. It is normally sharpened with a bevel on both sides.

WHITTLING KNIFE

See W–03 and W–04.
This is sometimes also referred to as a carver's number-one knife. The handle must be a comfortable fit for the user, and while the "fatter" handle illustrated looks unwieldy, for many people it will offer the greatest comfort and tool control. There is no right or wrong way to hold a whittling knife, so long as it doesn't end up cutting the user. It is essential to find one's own COMFORT ZONE.

W–04
One easy way to hold the whittling knife is so the thumb of one hand is pushing the blade safely through the wood away from the carver. See also the letter Q.

WIDE-BEAM LIGHTING

In the carver's context, a wide-beam light may be more appropriate for the workshop environment than a NARROW BEAM. A narrow light beam may be too specific and cause irritation to the carver. Before purchasing workshop lighting, check with the retailer as to the light coverage. Be sure to check the coverage, particularly if it is intended to use HALOGEN or other flood lighting or spot lighting, whether from permanently fixed lighting or portable "reading lights" for example. This information is often available in the form of a chart that indicates the spread of the light beam over a given distance. It is very useful information for the establishment of a lighting layout.

WINDING

See W–05 and W–06.
Winding is a form of WARP where the timber twists along its length, in much the same way as an airplane propeller. A board with wind is a poor choice for a carving panel, particularly if it has to fit within a frame. The test for wind is to place on each end of the board a "winding stick." Winding sticks are pieces of timber that are dressed so as to be identical in width to one another, and with both edges parallel.

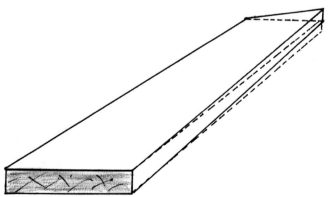

W–05
Wind is a common distortion in long board lengths.

WIRE BRUSH

See W–07.

A wire brush is a handy addition to the tool kit. It can be used for two purposes:

✔ If the wood to be used is rough sawn and has been stored outside, it may be full of sand or grit that will cause considerable damage to tools. A stiff wire brush is a very convenient cleaning aid.

✔ If the wires of the brush are stiff enough, and the wood soft enough, a wire brush can be used to add texture to a carving—such as a "furry" look. A good alternative for this activity is a rotary wire brush on a power drill.

W–07
The "furry" look on this carving was done with a rotary wire brush on an electric power drill.

WOODCUT

See W–08.

A woodcut is the same as a wood ENGRAVING. There are many different-shaped gouges for woodcuts, and they are generally small to fit in the palm of the hand and have a flat area on the handle to allow a very low approach to the wood.

WOOLLY

Woolly wood is similar to STRINGY wood.

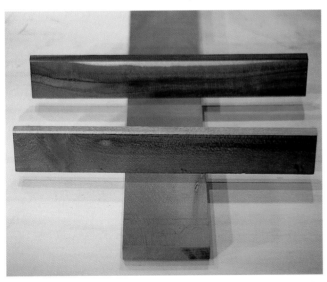

W–06
With a dark strip on the edge of one stick and a light strip on the other, it is easier to sight between winding sticks. If the edges are not in horizontal alignment with one another, the board is "in wind."

W–08
Many alternative shapes are marketed for engraving tools. Some metal engraving tools can be used with wood.

THE "X" FACTOR

Developing the mindset to ensure the successful execution of carving as an art form

The appreciation of woodcarving as an art form is certainly not a "new thing," as it is in most historical commentaries recognized as one of the oldest art forms of humanity. Bearing in mind that there were few other art media of consequence for early man other than colored earth and wood, it is not surprising that it has such ancient connections. Museums of the world contain many examples of very, very old works, and many cathedrals and other historic buildings contain priceless examples of early carvings.

Woodcarving in all its forms does, however, have a particular characteristic that separates it from the more "popular" art forms of painting, drawing, and ceramics. Whether it is relief carving (low, high, or pierced), in the round, or found wood sculpture, woodcarving is an activity where material is removed to create the art. In the others mentioned above, material is added to form the art. Woodcarving is "carving down," whereas most other art forms are "building up." This distinguishing feature has considerable ability to impart a fear and nervousness to the new practitioner, inasmuch as there is a confidence "barrier" built by a fear of "removing too much and mucking it up."

The new woodcarver is understandably tentative and often very slow. Both of these traits are perfectly normal. The new woodcarver needs to move through his or her fear barrier and gain confidence to achieve a successful outcome. It is this fear barrier that either discourages the interested person from experimenting in the first place, or discourages continuation. There are a number of things that need to be in place for this fear barrier to be removed. If there is a teacher involved, this person must be very conscious and respectful of the barrier, and empathetic towards the "hidden" needs of the student. An unsympathetic or ignorant approach by a teacher will do harm that may never be overcome. The comments here, though, will concentrate on the individual as a carver.

Do not be concerned by either slowness or nervousness. As we have already said, these are perfectly normal. To overcome both, it is very important that from the very beginning sharp tools are used. If there is any doubt as to the efficacy of the sharpness of tools, then every attempt should be made to find out if they are or are not sharp and what to do about it if they are not. Blunt tools will only create a situation of unnecessary and, more important unrecognized frustration, prolong the "tentative" period, and may give sufficient cause for the activity to be ceased altogether. Sharp tools are essential.

It is also of great importance to undertake the process of carving in the order outlined under the letter U. This order is not necessarily critical, but it certainly helps to get things into perspective. In addition, the questions and answers under the letter Q should be read. Once these "mechanical" aspects are covered, the rest is "in the mind."

Do not expect rapid progress in the beginning. It may occur, but it should not be an expectation. Take time to understand wood and its behavior. Time is the most precious asset of the carver—not from the point of view of not *wasting* time, but from the point of view of *spending* time. Do not rush. Carving cannot be learned "in a hurry." Carving needs and induces peace and quiet, is very therapeutic, and develops both a manual skill and a creative spirit both much glossed over in the modern world, although they are essential ingredients for human well-being. Allocate sufficient time to enjoy these benefits. If the time allocation is right, and the expectation is not too high, the first steps to fulfillment are taken.

The next most important ingredient for the successful carver's mindset is to stage the progression of the complexity of the projects so that there are no inadvertent quantum leaps. Ambition is one thing, but tempering it is the best approach. Whether carving in relief or in the round, the acquisition of tool skills and design interpretation can only progress at the rate of each individual's aptitude for, and acceptance of, them. It is generally preferable to progress from the simplest figure of leaf or animal by doing more of the same or similar, each time adding some detail or other design feature so that there is a cumulative learning effect.

Alternatively, move from one form to another at the same level. Try a simple leaf, then a simple animal, and then some experimentation with drift or bush wood to see what sort of shapes can be found. The development of the manual skill of applying tools to wood is as much influenced by time as it is by variety. Developing the habit of experimentation is discussed under the letter Y.

As time moves, and if this fundamental approach is adopted, the cumulative effects will be such that there will be a natural and instinctive growth to more complex shapes. Frustration will be kept to a minimum, time will be wisely spent, and development will be positive.

Visit art galleries, museums, cathedrals, and any other places where wood art is present. These are very important parts of the learning curve. The appreciation of what others do and have done is as important a part of the learning process as the actual doing.

"Y" NOT EXPERIMENT!

Experimentation exposes the benefits of always trying new things.

As we saw in the exploration of ways to establish an effective mindset for woodcarving under the letter X, one essential ingredient is the development of the habit of experimentation. If experimentation becomes an instinctive part of the carver's life, it will be amazing just what can be learned. One easy thing to do is leave in the glove compartment of your motor vehicle a regular 1-inch, slightly curved gouge. Wherever you are, and whenever you see a "new" piece of wood or

a fallen tree or branch, you can put the tool into it to find out what the wood and bark are like. Whenever you pay a visit to a lumberyard, always ask to put your chisel across the end of a rough-sawn plank to test it out. No damage will be done to the board and you will have experienced something "new."

Try pushing a gouge into garden loppings. Fruit and nut trees are commonly available, and there will be a large range of logs available for testing by contacting the local tree doctor or professional gardener. Knowledge is the greatest asset, and it is freely available, provided the will is there to find it. Look at the grain characteristics, and color, and search for any special features. Ask yourself questions: For example, is the grain rough, smooth, coarse, fine, wavy, interlocked, or brittle?

Experimentation like this can be extended to all aspects of woodcarving—starting with simple drawings and sketches. Purchase a small sketch pad and pencil, and take them with you wherever you go. At least sketch the profiles of birds, animals, and leaves. Collect samples as you travel and sketch them at home. Try copying objects from photographs. Simple animals and birds are good to start with. No one need ever see your drawings, so it doesn't matter how "bad" they are—it is the practice and learning that matter.

Experimentation like this will develop observation skills. Every time something new is tried, something new is observed—things like the grain characteristics in wood, the shape of the tip of a leaf, the shape of the eye of a horse. Many, many thousands of things that were previously ignored will be "seen" for the first time.

One of the best ways to learn observation skills for shapes is to purchase some modeling wax or plasticine, both of which can be recycled over and over again, and take time out to model different things that are of interest. If you have a yearning to do a carving of a dol-phin, for example, then make a wax one first. Observe the shape of the nose and how it relates to the forehead and where the mouth really is. Is a dolphin's tail vertical or horizontal? Observe and experiment!

The carver needs to experiment considerably with his or her tools. The best advice is to purchase tools on an individual basis rather than in sets, as explained under the letter Q. This is because each person has and develops different styles of work, and individual tool preferences are developed at a very early stage. In order to keep tool purchases from becoming an expensive affair, a high degree of dexterity and therefore versatility need to be achieved with each tool, and this can only be achieved by experimentation. It is important to find out just what each tool can do.

Try this as an exercise:

Take a 6 inch × 6 inch × 4 inch block of softwood such as jelutong (*Dyera costulata*), lime (*Tilia* spp.), basswood (*Tilia* spp.), yellow pine (*Pinus ponerosa*) or aspen (*Populus alba*), plus any gouge from the tool kit and a mallet. Secure the block of wood firmly in a vise, and proceed to dig a hole. In itself not particularly exciting!

However, here is what can be discovered:

✔ How does the shape of the bevel affect the shape of the hole that can actually be dug out?
✔ How does the diameter of the hole relate to the shape (the sweep) of the tool? Start with a small diameter and gradually get bigger.
✔ How is the bottom of the hole cleaned out?
✔ Is cutting along the grain different from cutting across it?
✔ Would a long bent or short bent tool be better than a straight one?
✔ Would grinding the bevel longer or shorter make any difference?
✔ Would sharpening a gouge with raked shoulders be any different from one with a square face?

And that is a list for digging a simple hole!

Experiment! Experiment! Experiment!

As experimentation with tools continues, and as subsequent experience is gathered, the size of the preferred tools will start to become clearer. Some people will prefer smaller gouges to do the same work for which others might prefer larger ones. Generally, there will be gravitation towards larger tools by most people; however, there are certainly no "rules." The choice of a mallet for most people will be a lighter, less "threatening" one in the beginning; however, once again most people will end up preferring a heavier one to that chosen at the start.

Experimentation with design alternatives for the same thing can be a major learning exercise.

A simple "S" scroll can be done as a plain "S," or with beads on the ends, serifs on the ends, or the "S" could be elongated or squat. Immediately here are five variations of the same thing, each of which could be done to look equally as acceptable, but each of which imparts a different flavor to the design. These design elements can only be understood effectively by experimenting with them.

Knowledge is the end result of an inquiring mind that experiments at every opportunity.

An inquiring mind experiments with different timbers, tools, shapes, and designs. The experimenting mind is prepared to have a go and "muck it up" and try again even if for no other reason than to see what happens. The accumulation of experience broadens the depth and breadth of knowledge and over time what seemed to be so foreign and potentially confusing becomes instinctive.

Experimentation will present many opportunities that otherwise might remain hidden or obscure.

ZONE OF COMFORT

The establishment of each carver's comfort zone is a prerequisite for successful development and growth. At the same time it can be a recipe for stagnation and boredom.

As we develop our mindset and continue our experimentation, so we begin to arrive at our comfort zone. Inherent within this, is a double-edged sword.

As the novice moves forward gathering the momentum of knowledge, soon he or she discovers that there really are no rules with woodcarving—with the exception of safety. There are some key principles that should be observed, particularly with regard to tool handling, but as for rules that must never be broken, there really are none. The timber used is what the artist chooses, the design is what the artist wants, and the end result is what the artist expresses. Of course some timber design and execution decisions may be better than others, depending on who makes the judgments, but this does not alter the fundamental concept that there are no rules.

As a general principle, the carver is within his or her comfort zone when there is equilibrium between each of the factors of personal skill level, the degree of difficulty of the chosen design, and the suitability of the timber. And because there are no rules, the carver will know when this equilibrium is reached, because the carver will feel "comfortable." Comfortable with the way the tools are behaving, comfortable with the way the wood is cutting, and comfortable with the way the artwork looks. The carver will be physically comfortable sitting or standing and holding the tools in his or her own way. The carver will be happy with the way the tools are cutting the wood. The carver will be happy that the design is producing the desired shapes that are in the mind's eye, and the carver will be happy that these are combined with the chosen wood to produce the overall creative expectation.

It is at times like these that the carver will experience the real pleasures of the craft—the perfectly relaxed feeling of escape from the rigors of modern life and the personal fulfillment that comes from the matching of expectation with achievement.

It is within such a framework that the carver will reap the best rewards of both the established mindset and the history of experimentation, and the best carving will be done for the skill level that has been achieved. When this equilibrium is reached, the carver should flourish, and the potential exists for the carver to be as prolific as he or she chooses to be. It is the perfect time to practice! practice! practice!

Speed will also increase during this phase provided the carver does practice. Things that may have needed thinking about will become instinctive—the order of proceeding, the choice of tools, and the sharpening of them. The direction to cut in the wood, the instant recognition of grain characteristics and how to handle them, and the flow of curves. The relationship between levels, the creation of smart shadows, and the use of undercutting for depth illusion. As dexterity with the available tools increases, the increased versatility will encourage more experimentation and more practice. The carver's increasing familiarity with the craft will pave the way for the development of a whole new set of skills.

It is this very familiarity, however, that may also be the carver's undoing. Too long in the comfort zone, and the carver may well begin to lose interest. This may first evidence itself in any one of a variety of ways, one of the most common being the use of tools that become more and more blunt. Or the carving that is never completed. There may be a general slowing down and it takes longer and longer to get through the work. Boredom has set in, boredom that will result in the cessation of the activity.

The individual will most likely recognize the signs of boredom. Once they are there, it is time to move on to new challenges. This may mean continuing with the same style of carving but increasing the challenge by attempting more complex designs. Alternatively, it may mean moving on to a new style. The technical demands of the formality of decorative relief carving could be relieved by switching to abstract, or carving in the round. Or using found wood to sculpture in relief. Try pierced relief for completely different effects to basic furniture decoration. Move to formal in the round from found wood. The important thing is that there is a complete change for a renewed interest and vitality.

Another good way to renew interest is to renew acquaintance with art galleries, museums, and exhibitions. Get out and about and see what others are doing and have done. Visit some great architectural monuments, or visit the workshop of a well-known professional.

Above all else, though, whatever you do must be pleasurable. Forcing the issue will only make things worse. The shifting of one's comfort zone to greater heights is for most of us best done in a gradual and comfortable way, so that we are effectively always within our comfort zone, but stretching it and moving with it to more complex, spectacular, and fulfilling works of art.

Add color with pigments and paint washes. Talk to other artists about how to do this—combining media is a great way to revitalize interest and create a whole new comfort zone at a different level. Remember all along the way that woodcarving is an art form, and as such should reflect the artist's intentions. There are no "rules" about art. That is its very nature. It remains the individual's personal expression, and as such should remain the art with which the creator is happy and comfortable.

INDEX

METRIC CONVERSION

inches	mm	cm
⅛	3	0.3
¼	6	0.6
⅜	10	1.0
½	13	1.3
⅝	16	1.6
¾	19	1.9
⅞	22	2.2
1	25	2.5
2	51	5.1

inches	mm	cm
3	76	7.6
4	102	10.2
5	127	12.7
6	152	15.2
7	178	17.8
8	203	20.3
9	229	22.9
10	254	25.4
11	279	27.9
12	305	30.5
13	330	33.0

inches	mm	cm
14	356	35.6
15	381	38.1
16	406	40.6
17	432	43.2
18	457	45.7
19	483	48.3
20	508	50.8
21	533	53.3
22	559	55.9
23	584	58.4
24	610	61.0

CONVERSION FACTORS

1 mm	= 0.039 inch	1 inch	= 25.4 mm	= 0.025 m
1 m	= 3.28 feet	1 foot	= 304.8 mm	= 0.305 m
1 m²	= 10.8 square feet	1 square foot	= 0.09 m²	

mm = millimeter
cm = centimeter
m = meter
m² = square meter